THREE
WOJEWODA
PLAYS

JOHN
WOJEWODA

First Montag Press E-Book and Paperback Original Edition August 2013

Montag Press 978-1-940233-03-1
Cover art © 2013 Stephen Brookbank
Cover design © 2013 Tara Odorizzi
Author photo © 2013 Stephen Brookbank

Montag Press Team:
Project Editor – Alexandra Polubiec
Layout Designer – Tara Odorizzi
Managing Director – Charlie Franco

A Montag Press Book
www.montagpress.com
Montag Press
536 E. 8th Street
Davis CA, 95616 USA

Montag Press, the burning book with the hatchet cover, the skewed word mark and
the portrayal of the long-suffering fireman mascot are trademarks of Montag Press.

Printed & Digitally Originated in the United States of America
10 9 8 7 6 5 4 3 2 1

MONTAG

This book is dedicated to Sophia Starr

Acknowledgements

A book like this actually represents years of work and I would very much like to acknowledge some of the people that were most important in its production. I would like to thank my friends Chris Gagoz and Elise Beauvais for introducing me to Charlie Franco. It was Charlie who took an interest in my writing. I would also like to thank Alexandra Polubiec for all the hard work and excellent suggestions while editing these plays. She really played a major role in bringing these scripts to life. I would also like to thank my brother Michael, my sister Nicky and my mother for being such enthusiastic supporters of my writing. I would also like to thank my son Jameson for being one of the best friends I have in life.

John Wojewoda

AMERICAN
BACCHAE

Characters

DIONYSUS
God of wine, ecstasy and ritual madness,
dressed as a Private first class

SERGEANT PENTHEUS
King of Thebes

AGAVE
Mother of Pentheus, dressed in leopard skin

SCENE I

Underneath an American flag stands DIONYSUS *beside a black trunk. He is dressed as a private, first class.* SERGEANT PENTHEUS *marches on stage carrying a severed arm.*

SERGAENT PENTHEUS

Yea thou I walk through the valley of the shadow of death, I fear no man, for the Lord is my Shepherd and the Lord has a cock! Yea thou I walk through the valley of the shadow of death, I fear no women, for I too, like the Lord have a cock!

(He throws the severed arm to the ground.)

I'll kill you! No questions! I'll bust your fucking skull and poke at your babies with the razor edge of your shattered limbs! You live in this world like pigs in their own vomit! You're a fucking pussy! I laugh at your thoughts! Your thoughts visit my mind at the exact moment they visit yours! Your head spins like a piece of fly shit hanging from a spider's web! You're a fucking monkey, making judgments! Fuck your judgements! You hide the smell of your own feces with perfumes you've stuffed with the rotted carcasses of the innocent lambs of the earth! Silence! No polemics! No eulogies! Just listen! I've been up to my neck in rotted corpses so long I smell like shit!

(He smells his hands.)

These hands have torn the limbs from those crass and bitter thugs some might call my fellow men. You do me an injustice! I am not a fool! I've reached like the mountains reach! I've strived and fought like a fucking rabid Hyena. I know! I know what God is like! I know that he's infinite, perfect and that he never moves or changes and that he has a cock! It's Him! He is the cause of all this shit! I'm a fucking holy man! It's you, you ferret-faced, pin-nosed little weasel! It's you who is the misguided one, the blind one! I see with perfect vision! I hear with pristine clarity! By ripping the eyes out of the stinking sockets of baggy-legged, moronic, asshole faggots like you, I've- let me see, how should I put it? I've accumulated vision.

(He spits.) Vision tastes like shit! It smells like piss! I fucking hate it! *(He picks up the severed arm.)*

You see this? Smell it! Eat it! It's fucking garbage! You see these, the fingers? They wasted precious hours pulling on a cock, lifting booze, trying to get into some bitch's panties! What about fucking virtue and wisdom, or the fruits of honest labour? Not this fucking queer! Not this one, or millions, billions of others like it! This hand serves itself best when...

(He clasps the hand to his neck like it is choking him. He becomes sombre.)

...like a gentle vine clinging to a rock. It was through this arm, not my own, that I sought my own destruction. I yearned for its embrace, waited like a pale and blushing teenage boy. Tears begged at my eyes' doorways. I trembled- like a woman. I reached out my hand stretching it as far as it would go. If only we had tied! If only we could have tied at everything we did, I would have loved him. Loved like only man can love God! But damn it, he won sometimes, the bastard! He got to the finish line before I did! He was better than me, at some things, and when he tried to pretend like nothing had happened, I knew, I had to kill him. So I ripped his arms off his body.

(He tosses the severed arm away.)

And don't you give me that shit! You're the murderer! Your every pos- session consists of the ground up corpses of millions upon millions of slaves! You arrogant shit stain! Who am I to judge, you ask? That's so fucking typical. Just because I'm not the highest and the best, you think I'm wrong? You asshole! The good are the minority! They are the fucking bed-wetters of humanity! I am humanity, not them! Wake up! You've plucked the eyes out of so many fucking corpses, you can see clearly now. Who is responsible for all of this? It's God himself. That fucking hard-on in the sky! He always gets to the finish line before I do! All my life I've sought to destroy that which causes hate! As a child I blamed individuals, as a teenager I blamed society, as an adult I blamed the rich and powerful; now I blame him!

(He points to the sky. DIONYSUS *laughs.)* Who the fuck are you? Who's there? *(Looking at the sky.)* God damn you, mocking me! I've held beating hearts in my hand! Smell them! Smell them!

DIONYSUS
I'm not hiding.

SERGEANT PENTHEUS
I'll rip your fucking eyes out! I'll rip your bleeding flesh so that I might expose your evil! I'll dislocate your fucking jaw and make you swallow your own fucking tongue!

DIONYSUS
If you're not with us, you're with the terrorists. *(He laughs.)*

SERGEANT PENTHEUS
I declare war on you! I declare war on God! God is a threat to all decency! All Law! Expose yourself!

*(*DIONYSUS *laughs.)*

Come out where I can see you! Come out where I can lay these hands on your flesh! Where I can dig these nails into your flesh!

(Slowly falling to the ground.)

Damn you! Damn you! Damn you! Damn you!

*(*DIONYSUS *picks up a tambourine and shakes it while dancing around* SERGEANT PENTHEUS.*)*

DIONYSUS

> *(While dancing.)* Dust you are and dust you shall be. Dust you are and dust you shall be. Dust you are and dust you shall be. Dust you are and dust you shall be.

SERGEANT PENTHEUS

> Soldier! Stand at attention soldier!

DIONYSUS

> Sir yes sir!

SERGEANT PENTHEUS

> I've declared war, soldier, on that shit-eating pipsqueak in the sky! Do you hear me soldier!

DIONYSUS

> Sir yes sir.

SERGEANT PENTHEUS

> Isn't that funny soldier!

DIONYSUS

> Sir yes sir!

SERGEANT PENTHEUS

> First I goaded him with insults, called him every name in the book! Isn't that ridiculous soldier?
>
> *(Pause.)*
>
> Isn't that ridiculous soldier!!!?

DIONYSUS

> Sir yes sir!

SERGEANT PENTHEUS

> I've challenged him! All my life I've looked for the creator of all evil! Sought to stuff his mouth with death! Sew up his lips with veins and sinews! I have finally pinpointed it! I've hacked my way to the top of a heap of corpses! Finally, through this long mad process of elimina-

tion I've pinpointed the cause of all evil. We cannot back down now, soldier! This is our last and greatest battle! Yea thou I walk through the valley of the shadow of death, I fear no man, because I too, like the Lord, have a cock!

(Pause.)

Get me my automatic, son.

*(*DIONYSUS *gets the automatic and gives it to* SERGEANT PENTHEUS.*)*

Shhhhhh! Be very quiet. This, soldier, is the ultimate battle. Wouldn't you say so? We have a retinue of spies, we got to send them all out! *(Laughs.)* They may never come back! I'm going to have to sabotage every bridge and destroy every building!

(Laughs.) It's absurd! I'm going to need bullets that can be everywhere at once and which can replace their own mass with instruments of their own destruction. I need bullets of inversion! Perhaps I should beat myself over the head! It's like one gigantic eye, soldier. One massive instrument of observation, like a huge Cyclops, even you soldier, even you. It's like I'm caught, stuck like a specimen in some bizarre sideshow. I am on display. I am the one object on display.

(Looks at his hand.) Even this hand, all part of an unblinking, indifferent gaze- we need a bomb that can cancel itself out, replacing the positive with the negative, leaving only void in its wake.

DIONYSUS
With respect sir! If I may make a suggestion sir!

SERGEANT PENTHEUS
Go ahead soldier.

DIONYSUS
Sir, may I suggest that since you are on display, it would be within your best interest to... well, to dress in such a way that would enhance your natural beauty?

SERGEANT PENTHEUS

> My beauty? What are you saying soldier? Are you saying you think I'm beautiful?

DIONYSUS

> Beautiful? Absolutely! As a matter of fact, with the assistance of a little inspiration, I think you could pass for... a woman.

SERGEANT PENTHEUS

> Do you really think so? I've always felt I was a little too brutish.

DIONYSUS

> Yes, but brutishness is so very attractive. Here, let me dress you.

SERGEANT PENTHEUS

> Dress me up like a woman?

DIONYSUS

> Only to bring out your more masculine attributes.

SERGEANT PENTHEUS

> Well, all right. But only if you don't tell.

DIONYSUS

> Don't ask, don't tell.

SERGEANT PENTHEUS

> In that case soldier, bring on the dress!

> (DIONYSUS *gets a box with the dress in it.*)

> Will it show off my back? I love dresses that show off my back, you know. I have such a great back! And I find those slits that expose a woman's leg to be so erotic. Tell me again soldier, do I look like a woman?

DIONYSUS

> You are so beautiful. I honestly think you are one of the very lucky individuals that possesses that allusive quality know as... seduction.

SERGEANT PENTHEUS

> You know, I've always thought so myself. As a child I used to look at myself in the mirror and pretend I could seduce the most timid and conventional of people.

DIONYSUS

> No!

SERGEANT PENTHEUS

> I have a particularly attractive bone structure, don't you think. *(Poses.)* Do you want to feel my muscles? *(Flexes.)*

DIONYSUS

> *(Feeling.)* Very nice.

SERGEANT PENTHEUS

> I'll tell you what I want. I want attractive athletic breasts. *(Putting on the dress.)* I want white gloves that go up to my elbows, you know the kind. I need a long string of pearls and black stockings. Can you get all that for me? I need a wig. I want to be a blond! Oh, I want to be a blond! Can you get all that for me?

DIONYSUS

> Yes.

> *(The box has everything in it.)*

SERGEANT PENTHEUS

> You know, I used to be a blond. I remember- they used to slow down when they saw me. Some would even stroke me on the cheek. I was often invited to sit on people. Did you know that?

DIONYSUS

> You must have been irresistible.

SERGEANT PENTHEUS

> I've managed to keep healthy. Health is so important to beauty. In fact, in my opinion they walk hand in hand. Did you want to feel my muscles? *(Flexes.)*

DIONYSUS
>*(Feeling.)* Oooooooo.

SERGEANT PENTHEUS
>I'd like to sit somewhere- just sit somewhere quietly and watch every-
>one admire me. I'd like to see that tortured look in the eyes of those
>who know they can't have me, who want me so badly they cannot look
>at me without blushing. I want to feel my body beneath my clothing
>like the perfection of smooth stone. To know that beneath this layer
>of cloth there resides a gentle miraculous paradise, a private garden of
>delights. I want to smell like roses and shine in the gentle sunshine,
>my hair down my back like the silky mane of an Arabian mare. I want
>to lie like a lioness in the lilies of the field, the rose of Sharon, on the
>lush green hills and valleys of paradise. I want to feel the weakness of
>love and passion possess me like sleep, which stalks as quietly as a kit-
>ten. I want each gesture, each footstep to resound like the fragrance of
>wind. I want my chalice to be filled with love. I want my love to hold
>me tight, to possess me in its mystical grip- so stern, so wise. I want
>my heart to be pierced with the sword of an angel, pierced like the
>earth by the sun filled with light, filled with sound, filled so that my
>lips might swell and pout and curl in the ecstasies of love's joy. I want
>to be held and caressed and fondled so that flames can warm this shell
>and my heart can open like the most tender flower. I want to roll down
>valleys and hills embracing the strength of love so tightly that it keeps
>filling me and filling me and filling me and filling me- so full I can
>only explode.

>*(DIONYSUS puts on a mask with bulls horns.)*

>Take me! Take me any way you want me!

>*(PENTHEUS falls to his knees.)*

>I'll do anything for you, just take me.

DIONYSUS
>You want my blood to fill your emptiness?

SERGEANT PENTHEUS
>Yes!

DIONYSUS

You want to give birth to a child?

SERGEANT PENTHEUS

Your child!

DIONYSUS

Your unspoiled virginity is like the earth. *(Puts a rope around sergeant* PENTHEUS' *neck.)* Imagine the earth at a different time- imagine its beauty. A mass of twisting vines and dense grasses and bushes, flowers of a massive variety in bloom, and nowhere, not a single path, not a single road or clearing. All of it alive and moving, circulating with the cycles of life, day and night, the seasons, a huge vibrating mass of fertility.

(Starts leading PENTHEUS *off stage.)*

SERGEANT PENTHEUS

The world before man?

DIONYSUS

No no. After the sacrifice of man, Sergeant.

(They exit.)

SCENE 2

(A phone is heard ringing. AGAVE *enters holding a severed head that is wrapped in a burlap cloth. She is dressed in leopard skin. We hear an answering machine answers with a* MAN'S VOICE.*)*

MAN'S VOICE
  Hi. I'm not home right now, but if you leave your name and number at the sound of the tone, I'll get back to you. *(BEEP.)*

AGAVE
  I want to tell you that I danced joyously! That the sun and the moon and the sky filled me with joy! That in this hurricane of madness, this chaos, there were crowds of happy revellers, drunk from the teat of a bull. We drank wine and broke bread so that we all mingled in sisterhood. All the women sprang from their frozen graveyard and we saw humanity as a fatherless child left alone in a strange world. I want to tell you how we all became the mother of that child. All our wombs together glowed hot with love, with joy, with celebration of a new life. We took the child back into our arms, back into our hearts where it again found warmth. And then the bull came down the mountain. Black, full of majesty and grace, its horns two tongues of fire, its hoofs made of gold, and it stood upright and took the child and reached with its hoof to the top of a tree and pulled it down, and it placed the child on a branch there and let the tree go and the child was gently raised to the sky and the women celebrated, screaming in frenzy. The child became a lion- filling the world with its roar- and our stomachs, gripped by such a mad craving of love- we could not resist the desire to eat the lion, to drink its blood, to let its flesh mingle with ours so that it would mingle with our wombs and thereby become eternal. The louder the lions roar the more irresistible the love in our stomachs drove us in frenzy. Soon the tree came crashing down. Never have I tasted flesh so sweet. All that was left was the lion's head, the trophy!

(She unwraps the burlap and reveals the head of SERGEANT PENTHEUS.*)*

From the very beginning I knew it wasn't a lion. I knew he was my son Pentheus. Every mouthful of flesh, every drop of blood was his. I saw the bewildered look in his eyes- saw the pain that only come with betrayal.

(Lights begin to fade. We hear the answering machine.)

MAN'S VOICE
I'm not home right now. Just leave me a message at the sound of the tone and I'll get right back to you.

(Lights fade to black.)

FAMILY WARFARE

Characters

SARAH
Female 60+ years old

MICHAEL
Male, her 40+ son

CORIN
Female, her 30+ daughter

VLADIMIR
Male, her 50+ Russian lover

Setting

Somewhere in America in a mansion there
is a large chamber, inside is a couch, a TV, a coffee table
and numerous chairs. The year is 2012.

SCENE I

Lights up on an expansive room with a high ceiling and a large wooden door- SARAH is sweeping up. Off to one side there is a couch, a coffee table and a TV. There are also a number of chairs in the space. MICHAEL sits on the couch.

SARAH
        Now Michael, don't ruin everything. OK?

MICHAEL
        What?

SARAH
        Be polite.

MICHAEL
        I always try to be polite Mom.

SARAH
        Yes. I guess what I'm saying is don't be controversial. No talking politics. I just want everyone to have a good time.

MICHAEL
        Well, it's hard for me not to talk about politics. I've been devoting my life to it. Am I not allowed to be myself? I thought you guys were doing this for me.

SARAH

> We are sweetie. We are, but it's for the whole family too. I don't want us arguing. I want us to get along for once. You have to know how much I love you darling. Now come over here and hold the dustpan for me.

(MICHAEL stands to help her.)

MICHAEL

> You love me; except when I voice my opinions.

SARAH

> No, Michael. I love you at all times. Oh, you look a mess. *(She fixes his collar.)* Now, then. Please, don't be difficult.

MICHAEL

> I'm not being difficult. *(He holds the dustpan while SARAH sweeps into it.)*

SARAH

> Thank you sweetie. Corin will be here soon- and you know how different you two are. I don't want you to argue.

MICHAEL

> So, what? Because Corin is making over 500,000 per year, all of a sudden she's right about everything? *(Empties the dustpan into a plastic bag.)*

SARAH

> It's not that. *(She continues sweeping.)*

MICHAEL

> Isn't it?

SARAH

> You should be proud of her.

MICHAEL

> Proud!

SARAH

She did it honestly.

MICHAEL

Honestly? She's a military contactor!

SARAH

So?

MICHAEL

That's not helping the world! You were the one who organized those earth-centered rituals when we were kids. That's why I've been protesting the Keystone XL pipeline Mom, to save the earth. *(He sits on the couch.)*

SARAH

I don't see why you should spend so much of your time worrying about a pipeline. Honestly.

MICHAEL

You just don't understand the issue, Mom. You prefer not to educate yourself because if you did, you would have to change.

SARAH

Nonsense.

MICHAEL

They want to build it across the Nebraska Sandhills. It's a sensitive wetland; and the Ogallala Aquifer, which is one of the largest fresh water reserves in the world- it spans eight states and provides fresh drinking water for over two million people!

SARAH

Oh, come on now. How would a pipeline affect an underground water source?

MICHAEL

Because of all the oil spills Mom! Not to mention climate change! This oil comes from the Alberta tar sands in Canada. It takes three barrels of water to extract one barrel of this oil. It's the dirtiest, the most polluting oil in the world! If it's fully exploited, it could ruin the climate for good.

SARAH

Are you sure you're not exaggerating a little, Michael? You have a tendency to exaggerate things.

MICHAEL

No. I am not exaggerating. I'm just telling it like it is. You know it was you, Mother, with your nature-worshipping rituals. It was you who instilled in me a love and respect for nature.

SARAH

I just want us to have a cleansing, Michael. Please, just do what I tell you and behave. We need this cleansing, as a family. Now, come over here and help me.

(MICHAEL gets up.)

MICHAEL

I need this cleansing. You cursed me. You guys don't agree with my politics so you put a curse on me. *(Goes over and holds the dustpan as SARAH sweeps dust into it.)*

SARAH

Well- we didn't. That's just not true.

MICHAEL

You cursed me somehow, with your Satanic rituals.

SARAH

Nonsense.

MICHAEL

Really? Then why are you doing this for me now?

SARAH

You asked us to.

MICHAEL

OK. OK. Yes I did. *(He scoops the dust into the dustpan.)* But why did you agree to it?

SARAH

We're doing this because we care about you. Yes, we. Corin loves you too- even though she has a hard time showing it. *(Pause. She examines his face.)* Oh, Michael, why don't you shave your beard? You would look so handsome clean shaven.

MICHAEL

I just don't see the point. I should really just leave, Mom. You know how much Corin hates me.

SARAH

That's the depression talking.

MICHAEL

No, Mom. No.

SARAH

Yes, Michael. Now come on.

MICHAEL

Ten years of grassroots activism- hard work building campaigns, talking to business people, to citizens- trying to stop the war. All in vain.

SARAH

Maybe the wars aren't all bad.

MICHAEL

What?

SARAH

Corin makes a good point when she says-

MICHAEL

No! I don't want to hear what Corin has to say! *(Goes and sits again with his back to her.)*

You were different when we were kids Mom. You used to talk about the earth. You used to say Satan's power was the power of nature. You believed in saving the earth.

SARAH

And I still do.

MICHAEL

But you don't have a problem with war?

SARAH

No.

MICHAEL

How can you not?

SARAH

Corin makes a good point when she say's that the economy is also important. People need jobs Michael.

MICHAEL

And there it is. Here I am unemployed, 42 years old. Poor, single and homeless.

SARAH

If you need money Michael, all you have to it ask for it.

MICHAEL

I've spent ten years trying to stop war. Ten years, and I have nothing.

SARAH

You can't say you have nothing. You have your family.

MICHAEL

Like I said, I have nothing.

SARAH

Honey, when you're negative you can always find bad things to think about.

MICHAEL
Negative? How else should I be?

SARAH
Can't you talk about something else?

MICHAEL
I'm sorry Mom. I can't.

SARAH
Obsession isn't good for you, Michael.

MICHAEL
Can I have a drink?

SARAH
Well...OK. I guess.

MICHAEL
Do you have any beer?

SARAH
Sure, I do- but you know we drink too much.

MICHAEL
OK. I know that.

SARAH
Well, OK.

(Leaves the room to get the beer. MICHAEL *gets up and turns on the TV while he waits.* SARAH *returns and he opens the bottle.)*

MICHAEL
Thanks. *(He takes a few big swigs.)*

SARAH
Vladimir should be here soon.

MICHAEL
> Your new man?

SARAH
> Yes.

MICHAEL
> And he's from Russia?

SARAH
> Yes. He is.

MICHAEL
> Well, naturally I'm happy for you Mom. He's a lucky man to have you in his life.

SARAH
> Michael. That's a nice thing to say.

MICHAEL
> You know, Mom, your rituals always inspired me.

SARAH
> You never seemed to like them. You used to say it was nonsense.

MICHAEL
> I'm sorry Mom. I've never believed in magic.

SARAH
> That's fine.

MICHAEL
> But now, I'm not so sure anymore.

SARAH
> Well, we'll perform a cleansing ritual for you.

MICHAEL
> To lift my curse?

SARAH
Honey. The only curse is in your mind.

MICHAEL
My mind?

SARAH
Yes.

MICHAEL
My mind- unreal. I wish someone could just change everything about my mind. I wish someone would just unravel it and put it back together so it worked right.

SARAH
Sweetie- if you need to talk, we can talk- about anything. I just want you to be happy.

MICHAEL
Happy? I guess I invested too much into my activism. It felt so important to stop the attack on Iraq, and now it looks like we might even attack Iran. I mean, it came to the point where I would have this recurring dream- this dream where I'm trying to block the machines- I can picture them now. Not people, just these huge awful machines. It was those machines...

(Pause.)

SARAH
Go ahead Michael. You can talk to me.

MICHAEL
They were the machines that I was trying to run away from when I supervised the pipeline demo and totally lost it. It was like I was on acid. All I saw were huge machines. It was like a nightmare, I couldn't see people's faces anymore, I just lost it. And look, now it's all over.

SARAH
You did what you could. But, you shouldn't work so hard that you have a mental breakdown. It's okay to be selfish sometimes, Michael.

Just relax, enjoy life a little.

(MICHAEL *finished the rest of the bottle.*)

MICHAEL
Can I have another beer?

SARAH
Sure. *(The doorbell rings.)* That must be Vlad.

MICHAEL
Oh.

(SARAH *goes to the door. Enter* VLAD.)

SARAH
Come in, Vlad. *(They kiss.)* Michael, this is Vlad.

VLAD
(Thick, Russian accent) Vladimir. Please to meet.

MICHAEL
Hello. *(They shake hands.)*

VLAD
Hello.

SARAH
You two sit down- please make yourselves comfortable. I'm just going to get some snacks- I'll be right back.

(*Exits.* MICHAEL *and* VLAD *sit on the couch.*)

VLAD
American television good. Is much better than Russian television. Yes? *(He takes the remote and starts surfing.)*

MICHAEL
Right. So, Vladimir. Do you mind if I call you Dad.

VLAD

This is joke?

MICHAEL

I guess. I don't know who my father is- could be any number of men.

VLAD

Your mother. High Priestess- you are lucky.

MICHAEL

So. You're in her cult?

VLAD

Cult? Da. I am lucky. Your mother- she help me. Very good.

MICHAEL

Very good.

VLAD

I have big muscles and she like these muscles. No?

MICHAEL

Oh God. So - what kind of work do you do, Vlad?

VLAD

I work security guard. I work for your sister Corin

MICHAEL

OK. I didn't realize that. OK. And how did you meet my mother?

VLAD

Here. At ritual- she choose me.

MICHAEL

Ya. Sounds like Mom.

VLAD

You, too- you are member of coven?

MICHAEL
No. No. I'm the rebel in the family. I grew up thinking it was all baloney.

VLAD
Baloney? What is Baloney?

MICHAEL
Baloney? Oh, it's actually a kind of inexpensive sandwich meat.

VLAD
Sandwich?

MICHAEL
Yes- but it's just an expression.

VLAD
It is, how you say, idiomatic statement?

MICHAEL
Exactly

VLAD
You mean, like bull shit?

MICHAEL
Exactly. Baloney means the same.

VLAD
...as bull shit.

MICHAEL
Yes.

VLAD
No. This ritual. No. It is no bullshit.

MICHAEL
No?

VLAD

    No. I make oath to Lucifer- and then, job. I get job. I come to this country as refugee, and I meet Sarah. She make ritual to Lucifer, I get job. Good job.

MICHAEL

    What part of Russia are you from?

VLAD

    Yokshar Ola. Town called Yurino. Small town.

MICHAEL

    And you are a political refugee?

VLAD

    Yes. I protest government corruption.

MICHAEL

    You are a protestor?

VLAD

    In Russia, da. Here, no.

MICHAEL

    You see, this is me. I'm a protestor. I protest here.

VLAD

    Here?

MICHAEL

    Yes.

VLAD

    But why you protest here?

MICHAEL

    I'm an environmentalist.

VLAD

    OK.

MICHAEL
Social activist.

VLAD
You protest here?

MICHAEL
Yes.

VLAD
Why?

MICHAEL
Why? Look, Vladimir. This capitalist system, it's unsustainable. Do you understand?

VLAD
You are communist?

MICHAEL
No.

VLAD
You are leftist?

MICHAEL
I'm a libertarian socialist, I suppose.

VLAD
Oh. No. This is no good.

MICHAEL
What do you mean?

VLAD
This system is no good. Is bull shit.

MICHAEL
Well, just because you're my new Dad, doesn't mean we have to agree.

VLAD
Joking. Da?

MICHAEL
Ok, so you don't understand the issue.

VLAD
Money. Only money.

MICHAEL
Money. No! You don't understand.

VLAD
Without money, no socialism, everything cost money. Socialism, is too expensive. Is no good.

MICHAEL
Yeah, sure, but there's more to life than just money.

(SARAH *enters wearing a bright red robe and a white ritual mask. She puts a tray of cold cuts and cheese on the coffee table.*)

MICHAEL
Mom. You're wearing your vestment.

(SARAH *walks over to the middle of the room, where a chalk circle will later be drawn, and turns and poses for a Moment.*)

SARAH
Yes.

VLAD
(VLAD *falls to his knees in front of her.*) I show respect.

MICHAEL
To her femininity?

SARAH
Exactly, Michael. To my femininity. Now then, get up off the ground, Vlad. Have some cold cuts and cheese, relax. We're still waiting for

Corin. It's been years since you've joined us in our ritual Michael. Vladimir is here because we need to balance things, we need two men and two women.

VLAD

Thank you Sarah, I am very hungry, but I am asking, may I have drink of water?

SARAH

Oh yes, certainly darling.

MICHAEL

I've been discussing politics with Vlad Mom.

SARAH

Michael, please.

MICHAEL

He was telling me that in Russia he was a protestor against corruption, so I told him that I was a protestor here in America.

VLAD

Is OK? Sarah? Is OK?

SARAH

Yes, Vlad. It's perfectly all right. Eat, eat if you're hungry, don't be shy!

MICHAEL

He was disagreeing with me. He seems to feel there is no need for protest, here in America.

SARAH

Michael– please, can we not talk politics?

MICHAEL

Not talk politics. Not talk politics. That's all I ever hear from you - from everyone.

VLAD

(With his mouth full.) I am not protest here in America. No protest.

SARAH
>No. Of course not Vlad.

MICHAEL
>Why? Because everything is fine here in America?

VLAD
>Is no like Russia. No KGB.

MICHAEL
>No KGB? No. Just big oil and CIA.

SARAH
>Michael. Please.

MICHAEL
>Please what?

SARAH
>Can't we talk about something else?

MICHAEL
>Like what?

SARAH
>I don't know.

MICHAEL
>You of all people should agree with me Mom. Aren't you worried about the environment?

SARAH
>Yes, I am.

MICHAEL
>Because big oil and the multinationals are a problem.

VLAD
>No. Muslims- they are problem.

MICHAEL
Baloney.

VLAD
Baloney?

MICHAEL
Look, Vlad, you know who Mosaddeq was?

SARAH
Michael, please.

MICHAEL
It's really important that Vlad knows who Mosaddeq was, Mom. In the 1950s -you know Iran?

VLAD
Iran is problem.

MICHAEL
Sure, but not in the 50's. In the 50's they had a western-style Democracy based on the United States with a similar Constitution.

SARAH
Michael, just have some cold cuts.

MICHAEL
I'm vegan now Mom.

SARAH
Vegan?

MICHAEL
Like I was saying, in Iran they used to have freedom of speech– an electoral system- they even dressed like Europeans. They had democratic elections, and in 1951 they voted for this guy, Mosaddeq.

SARAH
Why don't you eat cheese and crackers, Michael?

MICHAEL

No, Mom. No animal products. So, Mosaddeq in Iran, he was an anti-communist, free-market capitalist. He liked the USA- and when he took office he had the great idea to nationalize the oil industry. It was a resource on Iranian soil, but all the revenue was going to British and American private companies like BP and Exxon. Mosaddeq offered to buy them out, and seized the oil in the name of Iran. And the British and Americans didn't like it, you know. They had to control the oil.

SARAH

Michael. Please stop. We are not here to talk politics.

MICHAEL

So Vlad- no Mom, just one second- listen, Vlad, in the '50s, in America- the Dulles family- Dulles International Airport in D.C. is named after them, have you ever heard of them?

SARAH

Well alright, I do have a plate of vegetables ready- and I'll get you some water Vlad. *(Exits.)*

MICHAEL

Ever heard of John Foster Dulles?

VLAD

(Eating.) Dulles. No.

MICHAEL

John Foster Dulles and Kermit Roosevelt, Jr.

VLAD

Kermit? Like puppet frog, green?

MICHAEL

Yeah. Kermit Roosevelt, Franklin Delano's grandson. It's relevant to today. John Foster Dulles was the secretary of state under Eisenhower. His associate, Kermit Roosevelt Jr. was involved with the CIA when Mosaddeq was trying to nationalize Iranian oil. What Kermit the CIA agent did, with only a few million dollars- operation Ajax it was

called- using bribes and corruption, he was able to depose Mosaddeq-
they infiltrated Iran, spread rumours that Mosaddeq was a com-
munist- and since these techniques were new -people believed the
rumours– and Mosaddeq was deposed, he was put in jail. He actually
died in jail. In his place, the Shah of Iran, a non-democratic totalitarian, was installed. It was considered a stunning success by the Americans
because it was done so cheaply.

VLAD

Da. I remember Shah of Iran. *(Eating like a hungry body builder.)*

MICHAEL

But Vlad. Did you know that the type of police force used by the
Shah of Iran was new for the Iranians and for the Americans? It was
very much like the KGB. It was called Savak. They used secret po-
lice- torture- blackmail- terror- to command absolute control over
the population, supported and trained by the CIA.

*(SARAH returns, the mask off her face and on top of her head,
with a plate of vegetables and a glass of water. She puts them on the coffee
table.)*

SARAH

OK. Enough! Vlad, you can come here and give me a kiss. *(He gets
up and gives her a kiss.)* And now Michael -you can come over here
and give me a kiss as well.

MICHAEL

You're trying to change the subject.

SARAH

Well, it's a very depressing subject.

MICHAEL

True enough- but what if Savak was the kind of police force we had
in America?

SARAH

What if who?

MICHAEL

Savak, the secret police force set up in Iran by the CIA in the fifties.

SARAH

I don't know, but come over here and give me a kiss.

MICHAEL

No. I don't want to.

SARAH

Oh- come on now Michael.

MICHAEL

OK. *(He does so.)* There.

SARAH

So please. We're here for a cleansing ritual.

MICHAEL

To lift the curse you put on me?

SARAH

I have put no curse on you Michael.

MICHAEL

I'm sorry if I'm a disappointment to you Mom.

SARAH

You're not a disappointment to me. I'm proud of you.

MICHAEL

Even though I'm a failure?

SARAH

You're not a failure darling- you're just more emotional than most.

MICHAEL

Can I have another beer?

SARAH

Of course. I have to get something anyway. Keep eating Vlad, there's plenty more where that came from. Just eat, I know your hungry.

(Exits. MICHAEL *and* VLAD *return to the couch.)*

MICHAEL

As I was saying, Vlad, I think you're uninformed of the relevant history of North America.

VLAD

OK. I not knowing history.

MICHAEL

Did you know that Canada sells more oil to the USA then Saudi Arabia?

VLAD

This is good.

MICHAEL

You've heard of the tar sands?

VLAD

No. What is this?

MICHAEL

In Canada they have sands that are full of oil.

VLAD

Oil. Oil good.

MICHAEL

Not good for some.

VLAD

Yes. Sometimes is no good for victim, good for citizen. Yes? *(Picks up the remote and continues surfing.)*

MICHAEL

How did you meet my mother?

VLAD
> Here at ritual.

MICHAEL
> How did you get invited to the ritual?

VLAD
> Through friend of mother, Irina.

> (SARAH *enters with a large wooden compass which has a piece of chalk in it. She gives* MICHAEL *a beer. The mask is back on her face.*)

SARAH
> See this compass- it is the tool with which we will make the circle-the circle which is life and in which we all will stand.

MICHAEL
> So how did you meet Vladimir, Mom?

SARAH
> Here at our ritual.

MICHAEL
> By invitation only?

SARAH
> He was invited by Irina.

MICHAEL
> And who, pray tell, is Irina?

SARAH
> A friend.

MICHAEL
> One of your powerful friends?

SARAH
> From Russia, yes.

MICHAEL

You see, Vlad, mother only has powerful friends, because she's the High Priestess. I'm a little surprised a refugee like yourself would be invited.

SARAH

We made an exception for Vlad. He is a devoted believer.

VLAD

I believe. I am believer.

MICHAEL

A believer? Mom - do I have to become a believer?

SARAH

Yes. Of course. That's what this is all about.

MICHAEL

You mean- I have to believe before you can lift the curse on my life.

SARAH

There is no curse on your life.

(MICHAEL *gets up and sits on one of the chairs.*)

MICHAEL

All my life you've been the High Priestess and I've never been able to fully understand it. I mean, you always said Lucifer was neither good nor bad, that it was just the power of nature.

SARAH

Yes.

MICHAEL

And when I was a kid, it was just something you did. I didn't question it. When I grew up I saw that it was very unusual.

SARAH

I do what my mother did before me- and what her mother did before her.

MICHAEL

And Corin will become the High priestess when you die, Corin will inherit your power?

SARAH

I wanted you to go to Yale- but you didn't go to Yale.

MICHAEL

I didn't want an MBA, Mom. I didn't want to follow in your footsteps.

SARAH

So. Look at you now. You are homeless, poor, single...

MICHAEL

I've devoted my life to trying to do the right thing.

SARAH

I wanted everything for my children.

MICHAEL

But it was wrong. It was shallow. That's why I've spent the last ten years trying to fight the government.

SARAH

And what has it done for you?

MICHAEL

Nothing. It's done exactly nothing for me.

SARAH

Well. See?

MICHAEL

So was I wrong?

SARAH

Yes!

MICHAEL

I was wrong to care about the people of Iraq?

SARAH

    We must sacrifice care, Michael. Care is weakness. I worship strength. Power. I worship it- as my mother worshiped it- as her mother worshiped it.

MICHAEL

    But you're so sweet, Mom. I could never figure you out. I had to go my own way. Ten years. I've been away ten years.

SARAH

    Yes. It's been a long time.

MICHAEL

    The house looks exactly the same. *(Gets up looking around.)*

SARAH

    Not much has changed.

MICHAEL

    We're still rich, millions of dollars.

SARAH

    You know I love you. You've never had to think I wouldn't give you anything you wanted.

MICHAEL

    Yes. Oh, yes mother. Yes. A Ferrari- drums- holidays in Egypt, France...

SARAH

    Yes.

MICHAEL

    But none of it is any good. All of it is shallow.

SARAH

    Really?

MICHAEL

    I want something else. Something you can't give me. A happy world. A healthy society.

SARAH

Welcome back, Michael. Welcome home. It's all still here for you. You're room is still here - you can stay as long as you want.

MICHAEL

But you have to lift the curse.

SARAH

There is no curse.

MICHAEL

There is. You have to lift it.

SARAH

It's in your head.

MICHAEL

The cleansing ritual, the chalk circle- will that lift the curse?

SARAH

The curse is only in your head Michael. When you realize this, the curse will be gone.

MICHAEL

I tried so hard to organize those people, and no matter what- broken cell phones, flat tires, pens running out of ink, road crews blocking the street, car accidents, people losing important documents. I used to think, God hates me. God doesn't want us to save the earth. God wants to ruin the beautiful green trees and fields- to turn it into a sludge-ridden heap of waste. Then I would think- no- there is no God. Just like my mother always said. There is no God. It's just us. Just us humans.

SARAH

That's exactly what I've been trying to teach you Michael.

MICHAEL

And it started to be too much. I realized I couldn't win, no matter what, because I was cursed. Cursed! Destined to fail...and then I realized, it was you mother....

SARAH

No. Nonsense.

MICHAEL

You and your Satanic rituals.

SARAH

Michael. With this compass and Vlad's help, I will make a chalk circle. Vlad, turn off the TV and come and help me.

(VLAD *turns off the TV and they make a large chalk circle*)

Inside the circle is your family. Inside the circle is power. Inside the circle is comfort and security. Michael, come and join us inside the circle.

MICHAEL

Join you? Why?

SARAH

It's part of the cleansing ritual.

MICHAEL

I thought we were still waiting for Corin.

SARAH

We are.

MICHAEL

So...

SARAH

Vlad and I are in the circle.

MICHAEL

Fine. Enjoy yourself. I wonder what's outside the circle.

SARAH

Oh, I can tell you what's outside the circle Michael.

MICHAEL
OK. Tell me.

SARAH
Death.

MICHAEL
Death is outside the circle and I can't help but notice that everything is outside the circle.

SARAH
There are those inside the circle and those outside the circle.

MICHAEL
Vlad. I wanted to talk to you some more.

SARAH
Vlad. Set the four chairs up so they are inside the circle facing outwards.

VLAD
Da Priestess. *(He follows her order.)*

MICHAEL
I can talk to Vlad. Can't I Mom?

SARAH
Michael. You are being very difficult.

MICHAEL
I wanted to talk to Vlad about Savak, the Shah of Iran's secret police force.

VLAD
Savak. Da. I remember this Savak.

MICHAEL
A secret police force is made of tears and piss, isn't it Vlad.

VLAD
Sarah. He is crazy.

MICHAEL

Crazy! That's what a secret police force is. Like Savak in Iran- a police force set up by the CIA, by American corporate, political, capitalist representation. A police force set up by the CIA in another country. In this case Iran, not America, but Iran. You get a knock on the door, the phone rings, some plain clothes man- someone who maybe resembles your brother- he takes you away and tortures you, and there is no greater authority to protect you.

VLAD

Must be obedient to authority. How can poor man be free? No. He has nothing.

MICHAEL

Good question. How can a poor man be free? This is the question.

SARAH

Michael. I didn't make the world this way. Those who have no power are weak, and weakness is a sin against nature. Weakness gets what it deserves. Inside this circle, Michael, this is where power is, it's the power of family- outside the circle is only death.

MICHAEL

So, the people in Iran turned to the only thing powerful enough to do away with Savak and the CIA and the Shah. The radical Muslim movement. But Islam itself has its own kind of totalitarian police, because only this can fight such powerful forces as the CIA- so Iran goes backward in time, moving from a modern, democratic nation styled after the American Constitution, to a society where woman have to cover their heads and there is no freedom. All because of operation Ajax, all the current problems are just blowback from that operation.

VLAD

Oil. Good.

SARAH

Michael. Your whole way of looking at is wrong.

MICHAEL
Oh really?

SARAH
Yes sweetie. Yes.

MICHAEL
How so?

SARAH
First of all, this is America, not Iran.

MICHAEL
Obviously.

SARAH
And you have no idea what goes on in Iran. You don't live there.

MICHAEL
That's right.

SARAH
Vlad, stay in the circle. *(She exits the circle.)* Michael. You exaggerate the situation.

MICHAEL
Mom— you're outside the circle. That means you can get me another beer...

SARAH
Of course, dear. If you want one, I'll get you one. *(Exits.)*

MICHAEL
So, Vlad, you see- oil is the problem.

VLAD
No. Muslims are problem.

MICHAEL
Why Muslims?

VLAD

Because they live on land with much oil.

MICHAEL

Shouldn't they have the right to use the oil that is in their own country?

VLAD

Then Iran have too much power- with bomb- nuclear bomb.

MICHAEL

Power should be balanced. Too much power in one hand is not good.

VLAD

You are Muslim?

MICHAEL

No. No, I am not a Muslim.

VLAD

Then why you like Muslim?

MICHAEL

Because they are people with human rights.

VLAD

You are communist?

MICHAEL

No.

VLAD

Why talking of people?

MICHAEL

Aren't people important?

VLAD

If people important, take all you have and give to poor. Then poor people become rich people and steal from you.

MICHAEL
We're all pirates. Is that it?

VLAD
Da.

MICHAEL
Yes?

VLAD
Exactly.

(SARAH *returns with beer and four black candles. She hands* MICHAEL *the beer.)*

SARAH
Here you are, Michael.

MICHAEL
Mom. Vlad say's we're all pirates.

SARAH
Nonsense. If you don't want to have a successful business, Michael, you don't have to -but if someone else runs a successful business, they are allowed to. Vlad, take these candles and put one in front of each chair outside the circle and could you light them for me too please.

VLAD
Da. *(He takes the candles and does as she asks.)*

MICHAEL
Like the tar sands business?

SARAH
Of course.

MICHAEL
What if your business hurts so many more people than it benefits?

SARAH

> All business is like this Michael. It's not religion. It's about a business man or woman- she has an initiative, she works hard and makes a profit. It's selfish, and that's the way it should be Michael, because the alternative is communism, which is pure poison. I tried to teach you this, why can't you see it this way?

MICHAEL

> Imagine the experience of an Iranian citizen, from Tehran, living under Mosaddeq, participating in free elections, feeling optimistic about the future and the nationalization of oil -then seeing him deposed and jailed, the imposition of the Shah and finally Savak. Could this kind of thing happen in America?

SARAH

> I don't think so. No.

MICHAEL

> Why not. Look at American Muslim prisoners held without trial.

SARAH

> Those people are terrorists.

MICHAEL

> Sent to a jail where they torture their prisoners.

SARAH

> Michael. Enough. Do you want this cleansing ritual or don't you? I went to all this trouble.

MICHAEL

> I want the curse to be lifted.

SARAH

> There is no curse. If you believe that, then the curse will be gone– because, you see, it doesn't exist. Now, come on- enter the circle with me and Vlad.

MICHAEL

> I thought we were waiting for Corin.

CORIN
(Offstage.) Mom?

SARAH
In the ritual chamber honey.

CORIN
(Offstage.) Is Michael here?

SARAH
Yes dear, and Vlad- we've been waiting for you.

(CORIN *enters. She is dressed like a business woman; a conservative skirt, business jacket, heels.)*

CORIN
Sorry I'm late. Hello Michael.

MICHAEL
Hello.

SARAH
Well, Corin, we're almost ready.

CORIN
I see.

VLAD
Hello, Ma'am.

CORIN
Hello Vlad.

SARAH
I'll go grab your robe. *(Exit.)*

CORIN
Has Michael been giving you a hard time Vlad?

VLAD
    Michael?

CORIN
    Yes.

VLAD
    No. No.

CORIN
    So Michael, long time no see.

MICHAEL
    Ten years.

CORIN
    You look the same.

MICHAEL
    So do you- you look great.

CORIN
    I am great.

MICHAEL
    So I hear you have a new position in the corporation.

CORIN
    I control people, Michael.

MICHAEL
    Right up your alley.

CORIN
    Yes. It is.

SARAH
    (SARAH *enters.*) Now that Corin is here, we can begin. *(Gives* CORIN *a red robe and mask. Corin puts them on.)* Now, Michael- be polite. Let's not talk politics.

MICHAEL
Not talk politics?!

SARAH
No. Please- we are here to perform a cleansing ritual before the great power of Lucifer. First, we make the chalk circle. Then, two men and two women enter the circle, four corners representing Earth, Water, Fire and Air.

MICHAEL
And so you are saying, Mom, to me, that outside the circle is death?

SARAH
Yes- and inside the circle is life.

MICHAEL
OK- and so what happens if I enter the circle?

SARAH
Well- then we make an oath– join hands and chant to the power of Lucifer.

MICHAEL
What kind of power?

SARAH
The power of your family, Michael.

MICHAEL
Like the power Corin has.

SARAH
Sure.

CORIN
(CORIN takes the mask off.) Michael's giving us a hard time. I told you he would.

SARAH
Corin- be patient.

CORIN
I have been patient.

MICHAEL
So, I make an oath to the power of Lucifer, and the curse upon my life is lifted?

SARAH
As I've said- there is no curse.

MICHAEL
But there is Mom- there is a curse.

CORIN
So, Michael. Are you a communist?

MICHAEL
No. No I'm not.

CORIN
You're not sympathetic to Al Qaeda?

MICHAEL
Al Qaeda? Of course not!

CORIN
Do you realize you are an embarrassment to your family?

MICHAEL
Mom.

SARAH
Corin. Don't you start.

CORIN
Well, he is- you've said so yourself. *(She leaves the circle and removes the robe, throwing it on the couch.)*

MICHAEL
Is that how you feel Mom?

SARAH

No. I love both of you equally.

MICHAEL

OK. But am I an embarrassment?

SARAH

Michael. I don't always agree with you- with what you think- the way you see things.

MICHAEL

Well. OK. That's fine, but am I an embarrassment?

SARAH

No dear. No, I'm proud of you.

CORIN

Proud? That's not what you said to me.

SARAH

Corin. You must understand- he's your brother. You two have always been at odds with each other. I was hoping this cleansing ritual could bring us closer together.

MICHAEL

It was you, mother- you- who instilled a love of nature in me with your rituals. I don't understand how you can not agree with me. Don't you see? There are so many problems- ozone depletion, collapsing fisheries, toxic contamination, species extinction, climate change, weapons proliferation, bird flu, the aids epidemic, over population- don't you guy's see? We have to do something- all of us!

CORIN

You know Michael, you are a typical leftist liberal- you're good at listing all the negatives and completely ignoring the positives. What do you think no one worked to make your family rich? So you think it just fell from the sky? Do you think we didn't have to fight for what we have? You think it was easy?

MICHAEL

>Look, Corin- I honestly don't understand.

CORIN

>My company- we are a private company providing the highest quality security services to our clients. Do you think it's easy? A cake walk? I'm making lots of money, Michael, sure- but I've worked for it. I've made myself into something- what have you done?

MICHAEL

>I'm not saying you didn't work to get where you are, Corin. I'm just saying- don't you realize that oil is a serious environmental problem?

CORIN

>I completely agree oil is an environmental problem- but what- do you think things can change over night?

MICHAEL

>No. I understand that.

CORIN

>The corporate community understands that a technological shift is on the horizon. A clean, hydrogen energy economy.

MICHAEL

>Yes. Exactly. We can separate hydrogen from water just using solar power, it's a simple process. We could get as much hydrogen as we needed in a clean way. We could probably even run our cars with water, some people claim they've already done it.

CORIN

>You know, Michael, you are probably right, there might very well be a way to run our vehicles with water - but if you think people are gonna start filling up their cars from the hose in the garden, you have another thing coming.

MICHAEL

>What?

CORIN

> Yes. Water is going to be the next big commodity -and whatever the commodity is, it has to be regulated.

MICHAEL

> Water is free.

CORIN

> Rain water, sure.

MICHAEL

> Tap water.

CORIN

> Well, you see, ultimately, no.

MICHAEL

> But that's drinking water!

CORIN

> Those are our resources, and we won't have bleeding heart Socialist's moaning about human rights.

MICHAEL

> Mom!

SARAH

> I think Corin has a point Michael.

MICHAEL

> No. This can't be.

CORIN

> What do you mean it can't be? It already is. Did you pay for the municipal water purification? Did you build the water treatment plant? No.

MICHAEL

> Our taxes did.

CORIN

>Maybe. But we're going to purchase the water treatment facilities all around the world. Municipalities and state governments will sell them to us to reduce costs. We will own these resources. It's already begun in parts of the U.S. and South America.

MICHAEL

>Water is a human right!

CORIN

>Says who?

MICHAEL

>Say's me!

CORIN

>You? A wrinkled-shirt, scruffy-bearded hack? What? Do you think because you yell into a megaphone that it gives you power? Michael. You are powerless. You want to know who has power Michael? Those with guns and weapons and money.

MICHAEL

>I believe completely in non-violence.

CORIN

>Too bad. Because if you believed in violence you'd be a terrorist and we could throw your ass into prison, without even telling you why! You might not be an embarrassment to Mom- but you sure as hell are to me. You are not unknown to some of my clients Michael. That's right!

MICHAEL

>Wait a second. What?

CORIN

>Of course. I run one of the most elite security companies. Several of my clients are very much involved in the tar sands.

MICHAEL

>It was you, Corin! It was you!

CORIN
>What do you mean?

MICHAEL
>Flat tires, lost cell phone connections, break and enters, lost mail. The curse! It was you! The curse is you!

CORIN
>I don't know what you're talking about.

MICHAEL
>Mom! Corin's been spying on me!

SARAH
>No, she has not. Corin. You haven't been spying on Michael, have you?

CORIN
>Spying. No.

MICHAEL
>So you call it something else! Surveillance?

SARAH
>Corin?

CORIN
>What.

SARAH
>Tell me.

CORIN
>OK Mom. Yes.

SARAH
>Corin. That's not right. He's your brother.

CORIN
>So?

SARAH
Your brother!

CORIN
Do you realize that he almost ruined it for me? When my clients found out he was my half brother- I had to! And at my own expense! Anyway. We won, you lost, and I got a promotion. So everything worked out.

SARAH
Corin. He's your brother!

CORIN
So what?

SARAH
What do you mean so what?

CORIN
Regardless of who he is- he was in my way.

SARAH
He wasn't breaking any laws.

CORIN
Except the laws of nature.

MICHAEL
What laws of nature?

CORIN
The weak cannot control the strong.

MICHAEL
(To himself.) The weak cannot control the strong.

SARAH
Corin. I am not happy with you at this Moment.

CORIN

What? You're not happy with me? Oh, come on, Mother. How can you say that? I've embraced your way of life. I've kicked fucking ass-corporate ass. I've eaten my enemies, torn them up like rag dolls. I've risen to the top of my profession- I've earned huge wealth- and you say you are not happy with me?

SARAH

He's your brother!

CORIN

Yes. He is my half brother, but has he ever done anything to help this family? All he's ever done is bitch and complain- and then to become a so-called "activist"- my God. It's absolutely unacceptable.

MICHAEL

Corin. That isn't fair!

CORIN

Fair? What's fair? Is it fair that some dickhead with an army-surplus jacket and a megaphone can ruin millions of dollars of investments that my client has worked thousands of hours to secure? Is that fair? Why? Because a small community of Indians- no more than a few hundred individuals- they can sit on a resource worth billions and expect legitimate private interests to sit back and agree to letting them keep a highly valuable property so they can trap gophers? Bull shit! I can't believe what an idiot you are, you almost fucked every-thing for me!

SARAH

Corin. I don't care if Michael ruined things for you, he's your broth-er. He's your family and family is very important, dear. Without fam-ily we have nothing.

CORIN

I don't care.

MICHAEL

Mom. Look. Look at what you've created. Are you happy about this? I've always been nice to Corin. I never hurt her in any way-ever. I always said nice things to her- and she- she was always a controlling, smug, arrogant bully. I thought it was because of your Satanist beliefs, that you wanted women to have more power than men or something. I never raised my voice to her or anything! How is this fair?

SARAH

It's not, Michael dear. No. It's not. Corin has done a bad thing.

MICHAEL

So much for a cleansing ritual. What are you going to do Mom?

CORIN

(Corin goes over and slaps Michael.) Mom won't do anything to stop me, you asshole!

MICHAEL

Mom!

SARAH

Corin! Stop it at once!

MICHAEL

Just like when we were kids.

CORIN

If you think you can just traipse into my territory.

MICHAEL

Your room, your toys- your things. I always left them alone like you said!

CORIN

Of course you did. It was my fucking stuff!

MICHAEL

How's this fair, Mom?

SARAH

No. No. Corin- this is unacceptable.

CORIN

> What?

SARAH

> This is just not right.

CORIN

> How?

MICHAEL

> Do you even care about how I feel? Do you just want to kill me?

SARAH

> Corin. You have to apologize to Michael.

CORIN

> I'm sorry, Michael.

SARAH

> There.

MICHAEL

> She's sorry? Mom- you don't get it. It's not fair!

SARAH

> No. It's not fair.

MICHAEL

> But you're the one who inspired me to protect the earth with your rituals- you have to see, she shouldn't have tried to stop me!

CORIN

> Too late now.

MICHAEL

> I can't stand it anymore! Corin- you are mean- just, mean! You hurt people and you don't care- so- then- why- can't you see? Do you like that she hurt me, mother? Mother?

SARAH

    No. No. No.

MICHAEL

    Do you like to see me in pain? I came out of your body -did you want her to hurt me?

SARAH

    No. Michael -Corin was wrong, she did a bad thing.

MICHAEL

    But mother, the tar sands are also a bad thing.

SARAH

    The tar sands?

MICHAEL

    Do you just want power, Corin? Just that and that's it? Why? How about a nice clean natural environment? Clean air, clean water- Oh my God! Water! No! Mother - it's not fair! Corin has to promise not to privatize water!

CORIN

    I certainly won't promise that.

MICHAEL

    No! I can't stand it! You're ugly! The sex slaves and the war and the biological weapons! The wealthy class is preventing progress! Mother! Don't you care about the millions of starving people?

SARAH

    Of course, I do. Of course, I do. Corin, this is unacceptable.

CORIN

    Unacceptable? Bullshit. I'll do what ever the fuck I want to do.

SARAH

    No, you will not!

CORIN
>What are you gonna do?

SARAH
>I'll cut you out of my will.

CORIN
>You will not.

SARAH
>Oh yes, I will!

CORIN
>What? Bullshit you will.

SARAH
>Corin. I'm serious!

CORIN
>What? You've never threatened that before?

SARAH
>I'm very serious. You owe Michael an apology.

CORIN
>What? Why?

SARAH
>We need family counselling. Mediation.

CORIN
>How about Vlad? Vlad, what do you think?

VLAD
>Family fighting– family always have fighting. *(He goes back to the couch and turns the TV back on)*

CORIN
>Family mediation? Slow down now, mother. I'm willing to negotiate.

SARAH

> That's more like it.

CORIN

> I can give Michael one hundred thousand dollars compensation. How about that?

SARAH

> That sounds more like it. How about that, Michael?

MICHAEL

> I don't want your money. I don't care about money- don't you see? Aren't you hollow and black inside? Isn't it a meaningless, material existence?

CORIN

> Not at all. I feel excellent inside.

MICHAEL

> Nonsense. You don't. Do you have any friends?

CORIN

> I have lots of friends.

MICHAEL

> But real friends- people you can talk about anything with.

CORIN

> Of course, don't you?

MICHAEL

> OK. Whatever, but I'm your brother!

CORIN

> Half-brother.

MICHAEL

> OK. Half-brother. Which half Corin? Which half?

CORIN

> The cold half.

MICHAEL
> What did I ever do to you?

CORIN
> Nothing personal, Michael.

MICHAEL
> How can you say that?

CORIN
> It's just the truth. It's unfortunate that we had to conflict in our career choices.

MICHAEL
> I can't believe it! You are just a spy for the corporations.

CORIN
> Nothing personal Michael. Look. You have the right to forward your cause and I have a right to forward mine.

MICHAEL
> You should have talked to me, been honest with me. I'm your brother, for Pete's sake.

CORIN
> Half brother.

MICHAEL
> Yeah, well the two halves are connected, Corin. So, mother, are you happy with this? Are you happy with the way Corin has behaved?

SARAH
> No I am not happy with the way Corin has behaved.

MICHAEL
> But beyond that, are you happy with your family? Look at us. She doesn't even care for her own brother.

SARAH
> Michael has a point, Corin.

CORIN

Michael has a point? What? Look, Mom- I have no patience for weakness of any kind. I am on top and that's where I belong, and it's where I plan to stay. Look, I offered you one hundred thousand of my own dollars. How can you say I don't care?

MICHAEL

It's not the money! It's never been about the money. It's about family happiness. Look at your family life, mother. This is it. Vlad, my new dad. Corin, my evil sister. You, my Satanist High Priestess mother. And me, a failure. This is our family. Are you happy with this?

SARAH

Oh, Michael– well, you know, now that I'm in my sunset years- I do wish we had more happiness and harmony in our family.

MICHAEL

You can't support the privatization of water. Mother, no. People need water to be free. It's a basic human right!

CORIN

Nothing is free, Michael.

MICHAEL

Air, water and friendship should be free.

CORIN

Nonsense. You're just a naive, scruffy, whining, liberal leftist. Private interests own you and they own everything else too. Maybe you don't pay for your lifestyle, but millions of other people do. Look, Michael, I didn't make the world this way. I'm just a realist. I understand that there are masters and slaves- always have been, always will be.

MICHAEL

Mother. It was you who instilled in me a respect for the earth.

SARAH

Michael. You've never quite understood our form of worship. Yes, we worship nature - the power of nature. We do worship Satan but there is a little more to it.

CORIN

Mother!

MICHAEL

Mom, wait, no - are you part of the Illuminati?

SARAH

Well...

CORIN

Mother, don't!

MICHAEL

Oh my God, no. Answer me, mother– Corin! Are we part of the Illuminati?

SARAH

Oh, I don't know what's right anymore!

MICHAEL

Oh God. This is so much worse than I thought. It's all starting to make sense now. I had never even heard of the Illuminati ten years ago, but now it's all over the internet, and I've read about it, and-

CORIN

Now Michael, don't jump to any conclusions.

MICHAEL

Conclusions? I can't help but think of Savak- the Iranian police force under the Shah- before the Islamic revolution.

CORIN

Oh God. Michael, don't talk to me about the Islamic Revolution.

MICHAEL

I'm just wondering about how a police force like Savak, how does that kind of police force get started, get organized. It has to come from families on the top, from above, not below.

CORIN

Well, of course. Security is big business.

MICHAEL

You see, Corin- Savak was all about torture. They used torture- that is what made them evil.

CORIN

Nonsense. Torture isn't necessarily evil.

MICHAEL

We have to outlaw torture, Corin. You have poor values!

CORIN

Poor values? What do you, a twelve-dollar-an-hour hippy, know about value? Do you think your quality of life isn't the result of the success of the wealthy class? It is. Totally and completely. We make this county what it is, with the precious illusion of freedom.

MICHAEL

Illusion?

CORIN

Absolutely. Money is the only true power, Michael. No, you never did understood our rituals.

MICHAEL

Oh God. I've always been willing to accept that you had a different kind of belief system, Mom. A different way of worship- but the Illuminati- mother...

SARAH

Michael, listen. There is no soul. We live only once. Those who spin the wheel of fortune and win- they live the best life. That is what the Illuminati believe. The poor must have their illusion of God and soul to stop them from rising up. Meanwhile, the Illuminati have organized the greatest and most powerful people of the world since the 17th century. We run the world.

MICHAEL

> For years I thought you were a Satan worshiper. But you're too sweet, mother. You're so sweet. I was willing to accept you were worshiping Satan, but this is too much to believe.

SARAH

> Now Michael, do you really think it's better to have no power, or to have the most powerful power in the world?

MICHAEL

> Money? Is that it? That's all?

SARAH

> Molloch.

CORIN

> Mother! Be quiet!

SARAH

> It's too late, Corin.

CORIN

> Mother, you've just broken a very strict code of silence.

MICHAEL

> Torture? Corin. You can't defend torture!

CORIN

> Oh, I do defend it. We must always have torture. It is the sovereign right of power. We must be allowed to punish, repudiate and correct.

MICHAEL

> Then you're no better than Savak.

CORIN

> Nonsense. Obviously something as serious as torture must be regulated. Non-lethal intervention is what my company is all about. As a matter of fact, Michael, we are currently developing many new non-lethal technologies for sequestering and controlling.

MICHAEL

>Mother. Would you please mix me a martini?

SARAH

>Of course, dear. Would you like one too, Corin?

CORIN

>Why not?

SARAH

>Would you like one too, Vlad.

VLAD

>Da. Please.

>*(Sarah exits.)*

CORIN

>Vlad. Why don't you show Michael your new secret weapon.

VLAD

>Show new weapon? This is top secret!

CORIN

>Get off the couch, turn off the TV and show him, now! That's an order.

>*(VLAD turns off the TV, gets up and pulls out a small device.)*

>This device, Michael- you see, this device is a new, improved, non-lethal. It delivers microwaves that make the body feel like it's on fire. It's very painful, but doesn't cause any lasting damage. It's completely wireless and works at a distance of up to ten meters. All I have to do is point it in your general direction.

MICHAEL

>You don't get it. We have to resolve conflict non-violently- without war and without your stupid secret weapon!

CORIN

Wrong! That would mean the strong would become less powerful, and the weak would become more powerful.

MICHAEL

Yes, exactly.

CORIN

You want me to just give it up? Well I don't want to... and you can't take it from me, because I'm stronger than you- so what are you going to do?

MICHAEL

I'll sue you in court and fight you in the media! I'll educate and organize the people to change the laws. You can't defend torture!

CORIN

Vlad. Microwave Michael!

VLAD

What?

CORIN

You heard me, Vlad. Microwave Michael, that's an order. You are my officer, and that is an order.

VLAD

Da. *(Microwaves* MICHAEL.*)*

MICHAEL

Ahhhhhhhhhhh! Ahhhhhhhh! Ahhhhhhhhhhh!!!!!!!!

(SARAH enters.)

SARAH

What's going on?

MICHAEL

Mom! Corin microwaved me with her new secret weapon!

SARAH
> What do you mean?

MICHAEL
> Corin ordered Vlad to shoot me with her new secret weapon!

SARAH
> What?

MICHAEL
> When you went to make the martinis!

SARAH
> She didn't!

MICHAEL
> She did!

CORIN
> I did not!

SARAH
> Vlad!

VLAD
> Oh, no, Sarah! I am sorry. I am only do what Corin order- I am only following order!

SARAH
> Only following orders? Vlad- he's my son!

VLAD
> Sorry, Sarah. Please you not be angry!

SARAH
> Not be angry? You hurt Michael- on purpose!

CORIN
> It's completely non-lethal. There is no physical damage done of any kind. At a low voltage, this new weapon is perfectly safe.

MICHAEL
> It hurts like hell!

SARAH
> Vlad. I'm very unhappy!

VLAD
> No. Please, not be unhappy. I am sorry. I am very much sorry.

SARAH
> No, Vlad. Things were going well between us, but you can't be hurting my son.

MICHAEL
> Corin made him do it, Mom.

VLAD
> Corin make me do this, Sarah.

SARAH
> Corin. You are out of my will.

CORIN
> What?

SARAH
> You are cut out of my estate. You are getting nothing. Michael is getting everything.

CORIN
> Bullshit!

SARAH
> Don't swear at me, young lady!

CORIN
> What the fuck are you talking about?

SARAH
> You are out of my will. I've had enough. Michael has a point.

CORIN

What point?

SARAH

That family is important, Corin. You keep saying Michael is a half-brother. Well, he isn't. He's your brother. Grandmother made a big mistake joining the Illuminati. *(Takes off her robe. She blows out all the candles.)* I like the sex parties, but that's it. There's more to life than being a High Priestess. Look at this. Your own brother, Corin. I am just plain sick of the Illuminati!

CORIN

Well, I'm not sick of it! So if you don't want to participate, fine, but you can't cut me out of your will mother.

SARAH

I've spoiled you. I was wrong.

VLAD

Sarah. Please not be angry. I am make mistake. I like Michael. He is good boy.

MICHAEL

That really hurt. Just like when we were kids. She'd hit me and you were never there to defend me. It's not fair!

SARAH

I need a drink. I need a drink! I'm going to get myself a bottle! *(Exits.)*

CORIN

Vlad! Microwave Michael. Microwave him now!

VLAD

Corin. I cannot.

CORIN

It's an order!

VLAD

We must wait for Sarah!

CORIN

Give me the secret weapon, then. Give it to me! *(Takes the secret weapon and microwaves* MICHAEL.*)*

MICHAEL

(Writhing.) No!!!!!!! Please no!

CORIN

This is just the beginning, Michael.

MICHAEL

It hurts, Corin. It hurts!

CORIN

Take it like a man! *(Sarah re-enters with a bottle.)*

SARAH

Corin! Stop it! Give me that thing!

CORIN

No! It's mine!

SARAH

Corin, if you don't give that thing to your mother, I will cut you out of my will!

CORIN

I'm already out of your will.

SARAH

No, you're not.

CORIN

So, you're saying if I give you this secret weapon, then you won't cut me out of your will?

SARAH

Yes.

CORIN

Can I have that in writing?

SARAH

What?

CORIN

Look, Mom. I'll give you this secret weapon, if you give me, in writing, a declaration that you won't cut me out of your will. That's a good deal, I think.

MICHAEL

Are you happy mother? Does this make you happy?

SARAH

Corin. You are out of control, young lady. I am serious. Give me that secret weapon, or I'll– I'll smack you!

CORIN

No! Bullshit you'll smack me!

(SARAH smacks CORIN and takes the secret weapon.)

SARAH

Do you want an inheritance young lady? Maybe I should microwave you! *(Microwaves CORIN.)*

CORIN

Ahhhhh!!!

SARAH

And I'll microwave you again if you don't shut up and listen. *(Pause.)* I like this secret weapon. Corin, I have never hit you or caused you any physical pain whatsoever. I've hardly ever punished you at all....

CORIN

I'm leaving. Good-bye.

SARAH

Not so fast, young lady! *(Microwaves CORIN. CORIN writhes.)*

CORIN

Mom! That hurt!

SARAH

Corin. If you don't stay and listen, I'll microwave you again.

CORIN

Ok, ok.

SARAH

That's better. *(Turns her back. CORIN bolts.)* Stop it, at once! *(Microwaves CORIN.)* You get back over here, Corin!

CORIN

Mommy! No! No! No!

SARAH

I said, get over here! *(CORIN comes back to the circle.)* You like this secret weapon? I've never punished you. This is how it feels, Corin, when you microwave someone. *(Microwaves CORIN for a good while. CORIN writhes and screams.)*

CORIN

No! No! No! No! Mother, please! (...etc.)

SARAH

(SARAH finally stops.) That's what you are doing to people, Corin. Michael, take the secret weapon- you can punish your sister. *(Holds the secret weapon out to MICHAEL).* Here. Microwave Sarah for a while, I'm tired. *(MICHAEL takes the secret weapon. SARAH drinks from her bottle.)*

MICHAEL

I'm not going to microwave you, Corin. I'm going to talk to you peacefully, like an adult. You are wrong, Corin, about there being no physical damage- torture causes psychological damage, which can be easily argued as a very serious form of physical damage.

(Pause.)

You have no idea how much I want to change you. I know you hate me and you're angry at life.

CORIN
I'm not angry at life.

MICHAEL
OK. Listen. I love you, Corin. I love you, and you know why? Because you're my sister and I love you.

CORIN
Half-sister.

MICHAEL
Which half?

CORIN
The cold half.

MICHAEL
Mom!

SARAH
Corin. Are you not understanding? We are your family!

CORIN
Vlad, too?

SARAH
Yes!

VLAD
Oh, my Priestess! *(Goes to her and kisses her hand.)*

SARAH
I wanted to announce to you, Corin- and to you, Michael- that Vlad and I, we are fairly serious about each other.

CORIN
Congratulations, Vlad. My mother just saved your ass.

VLAD

Corin. Your mother and I- we are boyfriend and girlfriend.

CORIN

Oh. Well- you see Vlad, I thought so, but, you know, with my mother, you never know. She has had quite a few "boyfriends."

SARAH

I'm sorry, Corin.

CORIN

Don't be sorry. You see, Vlad- I don't know who my father is.

MICHAEL

I don't know who my father is either.

SARAH

Well, things are different now. I realize I've made some mistakes- you see, we have these sex parties with doctors present and everyone checked out for STDs and birth control paid for. Well, taking it was my own responsibility...

MICHAEL

OK. So are you happy with that life?

SARAH

No. I'm not. I've come to realize that family is the most important. I think I know who your father is, Michael. But I've never had the courage to tell you.

MICHAEL

What?

SARAH

Yes.

MICHAEL

Who?

SARAH
>   You'd never believe it.

MICHAEL
>   Who?

SARAH
>   Henry Kissinger.

MICHAEL
>   Oh my God, no! Oh, God, no. No! No!

SARAH
>   I know it sounds absurd, but you see– we are ridiculous. I see that now. Corin, do you see?

CORIN
>   And do you know who my father is?

SARAH
>   That I don't know.

CORIN
>   Oh, great! Michael's father is Henry Kissinger and my father- who knows! Some guy in a mask at an orgy! That's just fucking great! Henry Kissinger? Holy fuck! Are you sure, Mom, you don't have it backwards? Surely my father is Henry Kissinger- my father is Henry Kissinger!

MICHAEL
>   Oh, God. This is horrible! I hate him!

CORIN
>   Surely Michael's father was a guy in a mask at an orgy and my father is Henry Kissinger! I want Henry Kissinger. I want that! Why can't you tell me my father is Henry Kissinger! So you're saying my father is a guy in a mask at an orgy and Michael's father is Henry fucking Kissinger?

SARAH
>   Well, Henry Kisinger was wearing a mask, too.

CORIN

I hate you! You make me sick! You think Michael is so special? So his father is Henry Kissinger? You're just a slut! You're stupid! I want my secret weapon back, now! *(Lunges at* MICHAEL *and grabs the secret weapon. Starts microwaving* MICHAEL.*)*

SARAH

Corin! No! Give me that secret weapon!

CORIN

No!

SARAH

Corin! Give it!

*(*CORIN *points the secret weapon at* SARAH.*)*

You'd microwave your own mother?

CORIN

I'd microwave anybody! I'd microwave the fucking President if I had to- so back off, Mom!

SARAH

You would not!

CORIN

Back off! I'd microwave you and the whole fucking Chicago Bears football team. I'd microwave the fucking mayor- and I'll microwave the fucking shit out of you, Mom.

*(*VLAD *subdues* CORIN, *gets the secret weapon and microwaves* CORIN.*)*

SARAH

Vlad! Stop microwaving my daughter!

VLAD

Sorry! I am only helping!

SARAH

If anybody microwaves my daughter, it's me- or Michael, I guess. Here, Michael. *(Gives* MICHAEL *the secret weapon.)* How dare you threaten me, Corin? Your own mother!

CORIN

I'm sorry.

SARAH

What?

CORIN

I'm sorry. OK? I'm sorry- you can't expect me to be somebody else, Mother- all of my life you've wanted me to be a high-powered business executive -and now you tell me Henry Kissinger is Michael's dad and that my dad is some guy in a mask at an orgy.

MICHAEL

Are you still willing to defend torture, Corin?

SARAH

Yes. Are you still willing to defend torture Corin?

MICHAEL

Are you still unable to have respect for your own family?

SARAH

Yes. Are you still unable to have respect for your own family?

MICHAEL

Family is important, Corin.

SARAH

Yes. Family is important, Corin.

MICHAEL

I love you. I know you find it hard to believe.

SARAH

Michael loves you. I know you find it hard to believe.

MICHAEL
   Mother. Please.

SARAH
   "Mother. Please." What?

MICHAEL
   You're repeating everything I say. Would you please stop, mother?
   (He mistakenly microwaves SARAH.*)*

SARAH
   Ahhhhh!!!

MICHAEL
   Oh- darn it. Sorry Mom. Are you okay? *(Drops the secret weapon and goes to help.)*

SARAH
   What the hell was that Michael!

MICHAEL
   Sorry. That was a total mistake. *(*CORIN *picks up the secret weapon and microwaves* VLAD.*)*

VLAD
   Ahhhh!!!!

CORIN
   That's what you get, Vlad- you don't fucking microwaving me.

SARAH
   Corin!

CORIN
   Stay back, Mother!

SARAH
   Corin. I know you won't microwave me.

SARAH

Oh, won't I?

SARAH

Give me the secret weapon, Corin.

CORIN

I'd microwave fucking Angelina Jolie and Brad Pitt if I had to. If I'd micro-wave Brangelina Mom- you don't think I'd microwave you? I'd microwave fucking Mother Teresa, which means I would certainly microwave you, Mother. I'd microwave fucking Brangelina, Mom- so stay back!

SARAH

I don't believe it.

CORIN

Don't come any closer, Mom. I'm warning you!

SARAH

You're microwave happy!

CORIN

I love this secret weapon, you can't have it.

SARAH

You're not even a real police officer.

CORIN

Don't say that! We're better than police officers!

SARAH

You run a private security firm and you're microwave happy. It's not right. Michael has a point.

CORIN

Michael! You mean Mr. Kissinger over there? I'd microwave him and I'll fucking microwave you, Mom!

SARAH

You wouldn't dare!

CORIN
> Stay back!

SARAH
> Give me that secret weapon!

CORIN
> No!

SARAH
> Corin. Give it to me. Now! *(She takes the secret weapon.* CORIN *doesn't resist.)*

CORIN
> What? I...what?

MICHAEL
> This is how Savak started. A private security firm contracted by the CIA, started by some dysfunctional family.

CORIN
> I can't believe it. I didn't microwave you.

SARAH
> Of course you didn't. How could you microwave your own mother?

CORIN
> But... now I don't have my secret weapon anymore.

SARAH
> That's right. I'm giving it back to Vlad.

CORIN
> That means I have a weakness. My mother is my weakness.

MICHAEL
> Your family- not just your mother, but your brother, too.

CORIN
> Brother. You mean half-brother.

MICHAEL

Half-brother? No. Whole brother?

CORIN

Whole brother?

MICHAEL

Yes. Whole brother who loves you with his whole heart.

CORIN

Loves me?

MICHAEL

Yes. It's hard, but I do. I always have.

CORIN

Always have?

MICHAEL

Don't I always wish you a happy birthday- even though you never do for me. Don't I?

CORIN

Yes.

MICHAEL

And don't I always send you a Christmas card -even though you never send me one?

CORIN

Yes. But I'm a Satanist, I don't celebrate Christmas.

MICHAEL

OK, but when we were little, didn't I always respect your requests for privacy.

CORIN

Yes.

MICHAEL
> Do you know why?

CORIN
> Because you're a pussy?

MICHAEL
> No.

CORIN
> Because you're naive?

MICHAEL
> Wrong again.

CORIN
> Because you're afraid of my superiority over you?

MICHAEL
> Nope.

CORIN
> Then, why?

MICHAEL
> Because, Corin. I want you to like me. You're my sister- and for all your faults, I think you're a good person inside. You're only problem is you've been spoiled rotten.

CORIN
> How can you like me? I've only ever been a bitch to you.

MICHAEL
> Not always. Not that summer at the riding school.

CORIN
> Yeah. We had fun that summer.

MICHAEL
> We'd take that big black racehorse down to the swimming hole and

go swimming with it. Remember that? That was fun watching that great big horse swimming in the water. Remember? We'd play together with that big horse running around and we'd dive off the dock, and we played like we were scuba diving. You were Jacques Cousteau, and I was Falco. Remember? Didn't you like me then?

CORIN

Yes. I guess. Yes. I guess I did.

MICHAEL

What happened?

CORIN

You know, I haven't thought about that for years.

MICHAEL

You haven't? Well, I have. I know what happened. That following school year was the first time we found out about the orgies.

CORIN

Oh, yeah.

MICHAEL

And ever since you've been mean and bitter. Remember?

CORIN

I guess you're right.

MICHAEL

But I've always wanted you and me to just be friends- like we were that summer.

CORIN

You and me? Friends?

MICHAEL

Yes, Corin. That's what's supposed to happen with siblings. It's supposed to be pleasant. You're not supposed to spy on your own brother and ruin his life for the sake of money and power.

CORIN

I guess not.

MICHAEL

What's the Illuminati offering you really, Corin? I mean, is it worth it really?

CORIN

What's the Illuminati offering me?

MICHAEL

Yes.

CORIN

Unlimited power over millions of souls, I guess.

MICHAEL

Trust me, Corin. That's way over rated. Trust me. It wouldn't make you happy.

CORIN

You don't think?

MICHAEL

No.

CORIN

Come on, Michael. Unlimited power over millions of souls? Who wouldn't like that?

MICHAEL

What? To control their water- so that the only water they own is their own tears? That's gonna make you feel miserable, Corin.

CORIN

You think so?

MICHAEL

Absolutely. And torture? You can't seriously justify torture.

CORIN

It's just a little water boarding, a little sexual humiliation- the Barney song over and over and over....

MICHAEL

The Barney song over and over?

CORIN

I love you, and you love me, we're a happy family...

MICHAEL

That's twisted, Corin. And so is corporate spying. You should have spoken with me directly, that would have been fair.

CORIN

You wouldn't have listened.

MICHAEL

So, what? Throw me in prison without any charges? Water board me and play the Barney song?

CORIN

Yeah.

MICHAEL

Corin- that's just really, really strange. Does your company really do that to people?

CORIN

Well... Yeah, but not here in America. In Poland.

MICHAEL

Poland?

CORIN

Yeah, it's really cheap to do it there. We save like twenty percent.

MICHAEL

Oh God. Secret prisons run by private companies in foreign countries. How did we get to this?

CORIN

(Sings.) "I love you, you love me, we're a happy family......."

MICHAEL

And you don't think a police force like Savak could exist here in America, Mother? Look, they're already here!

SARAH

Michael is right, Corin. Michael is right! I'm quitting the Illuminati. No more red robes. No more orgies. No more blood sacrifice beef cattle barbecue parties. I'm through!

VLAD

You are quitting Sarah?

MICHAEL

Excellent, mother. Very good. Look, Corin- mother is quitting the Illuminati, so should you.

CORIN

Yeah, well, it's not so cut and dry. You can't just quit the Illuminati. It's the Illuminati, for fuck's sake, this isn't the fucking Rotary club!

MICHAEL

Sure you can.

CORIN

No. You don't understand. You can't just quit the Illuminati like it's the fucking girl scouts.

MICHAEL

It doesn't matter.

CORIN

It doesn't matter? What the fuck do you, a granola-munching hippy, know about secret societies? Do you realize how widespread espionage is? All major corporations and all major nations have spies. The CIA has its operatives in all major media outlets around the world, in all municipal governments. And so does China, probably.

And Russia, and Britain and France. And they're all paid very well,
I'll have you know, under the table, tax-free.

MICHAEL

Oh, God. It's so completely corrupt.

CORIN

You can't stop it, Michael, so you have to choose sides.

MICHAEL

Not true. We can tell the people.

CORIN

Go ahead. The people don't care. Tell them all you like. Most won't
believe you. It's all hidden in plain view as they say.

MICHAEL

Corin. You know what would make you happy? A healthy, normal
family. That's what.

CORIN

It's way too late for that.

MICHAEL

No, it's not. Look, you know why you became so bitter and grumpy
after we found out about the orgies and stuff? Because you wished
we could just be a normal family with normal friends doing normal
things, like birthdays and Christmas and stuff- didn't you wish we had
a dad? And that we could just be a normal, regular family?

CORIN

I guess, sometimes.

SARAH

It's all my fault. *(Sits in a chair.)*

MICHAEL

Well, we have a second chance now. Look at us. Me, you, Mom and
Vlad. Don't you wish it could just be domestic bliss- like a real, normal family?

SARAH

Yes. Yes, I do wish for that. What do you think, Vlad?

VLAD

Family? Da, rich family- this best way to be. Rich with much power.

MICHAEL

But what about love?

VLAD

Love?

MICHAEL

What about love? Do you have a family, Vlad?

VLAD

Family. You ask if I have family. I am not orphan.

MICHAEL

Do you love my mother? Well, do you?

VLAD

Love?

MICHAEL

Yes, Vlad. Do you love my mother?

VLAD

I can ask you, Sarah, same question? Do you love me?

SARAH

Do I....

VLAD

Well. So.

SARAH

I've never felt this way before. I've never wanted a steady boyfriend before. I wouldn't want to lose you, Vlad. I would never want to lose you.

VLAD
>Really?

SARAH
>Yes.

MICHAEL
>But, do you love him, Mother?

SARAH
>I'm so ashamed.

MICHAEL
>About what?

SARAH
>I've had so many different men- but never loved any of them.

MICHAEL
>But, Mother. Do you love Vlad?

SARAH
>Yes. Yes, I do.

VLAD
>What?

SARAH
>I do. I love you Vlad.

VLAD
>You? How you? You love me?

SARAH
>I love you with my whole heart.

VLAD
>No.

SARAH

Yes, Vlad. There's something about you. Oh it's not just your muscles and your huge endowment.

MICHAEL

We get it Mom.

SARAH

No. It's not just that. It's something else, Vlad. It's you. It's the way you smile. The way you look when you're listening. I think about you all the time. I can't wait for us to be alone together.

VLAD

Oh, Sarah. Sarah.

SARAH

The way you say my name. That sexy Russian accent.

VLAD

Oh, Sarah.

SARAH

When our lips touch, I feel something go through my whole body. And your eyes, Vlad- they are so deep. Something about them. Some deep longing in your soul.

VLAD

Sarah. No.

SARAH

I was hoping that today, you would meet my children- that we would come together. As a family.

VLAD

As family?

SARAH

Yes. That we could all be together. Michael has returned after ten years. Corin, well you know her.

CORIN
> This is bullshit.

MICHAEL
> Come on, Vlad. Make this a happy ending. What do you say?

VLAD
> I cannot say.

MICHAEL
> Come on, Vlad. Do you love my mother? Do you?

SARAH
> Yes, Vlad. Do you feel the same? Do you feel the same for me, Vlad?

VLAD
> You do not know me, Sarah.

SARAH
> What do you mean? You have a past? Well, so do I.

VLAD
> No, Sarah. You do not understand.

SARAH
> *(Falls to her knees)* I don't care, Vlad! It's the chemistry. You are the most beautiful man I've ever met. You've totally enslaved me. I know I act like I have all the power, but Vlad, I have no power. I am a slave to you. I couldn't live without you. I love you. I love you! Do you hear me?

VLAD
> Sarah.

SARAH
> Tell me you feel the same. Let me hear the words I long to hear.

VLAD
> Sarah. You do not know me.

SARAH

I know you. I know your body. Your shoulders, your smouldering eyes, your powerful arms, your gorgeous thighs, your huge-

MICHAEL

Mom! Stop!

VLAD

(Lifts Sarah to her feet) My name is not Vlad.

SARAH

I don't care if your name is or isn't Vlad.

CORIN

What do you mean your name is not Vlad?

MICHAEL

Who cares what his name is, Corin. This is something special.

CORIN

No. Wait a minute, Mr. Kissinger. This is fucking bullshit. I did a thorough background check on Vlad.

MICHAEL

Corin. Back off. Just back off on this.

CORIN

No. If Vlad is not his real name then he has a rock solid false identity. I did a top quality background check. What do you mean your name is not Vlad?

VLAD

You are poor, poor people. I sorry I have to be one.

CORIN

What are you talking about?

VLAD

Sarah. I want that you know. I love you.

SARAH

> For real?

VLAD

> For real, Sarah. *(They kiss passionately.)* I love you. I dream we be happy- as if we be like happy family. Like normal people.

SARAH

> Oh yes, Vlad. Yes.

VLAD

> Like I am be simple, working man. And we come home to home-cooked meal. And you, me, kids on couch, we sit and watch American Idol.

SARAH

> Yes, Vlad. Yes. You, me, kids watch American Idol.

MICHAEL

> What do you think, Corin? Wouldn't that be nice? To just be a normal, hard-working family, to not have to torture people, to not be full of anger and resentment towards your brother?

CORIN

> This is bullshit, Michael.

MICHAEL

> Come on, Corin.

CORIN

> You have lost your mind, Mother?

SARAH

> Corin. You are impossible. Don't you understand?

CORIN

> No, Mother. You don't understand! Who are you, Vlad?

VLAD

> Sarah. If I tell you truth- truth about my life- you will still love?

SARAH

> Yes, Vlad. Yes.

VLAD

> I am international spy.

SARAH

> A Russian spy?

VLAD

> Once, but now no. Now, I am work for world emperor- secret emperor- most powerful man. You have never met– is top rank Illuminati. He know that you are soon to quit.

SARAH

> Oh, Vlad. That really turns me on.

VLAD

> You people, in America, are like little children. You not knowing what world truly is. In Russia, I join KGB, young man. My teacher, Iosif Grigulevich, master of impersonation, specialist in sabotage, assassination- also make career academic writer on Latin America. Yuri Andrapov was my chief- Vladimir Putin, my enemy.

CORIN

> You motherfucker!

VLAD

> I am sent to spy on you.

CORIN

> Why?

VLAD

> Why? What difference why? Now all is over. You ask if I have family. I have son, two daughters- will be protected now that I am fulfill final order.

CORIN

> What final fucking order is that, Vlad?

VLAD

> To immolate house. Sarah, Corin, Michael, myself- in news will say mass suicide of Satanic cult. Cannot quit Illuminati. Corin is correct. I have listening device in filling of teeth. There are explosives in house. We cannot escape. Do you still love me?

SARAH

> Just kiss me, Vlad. *(They kiss as the world turns to fire.)*

CORIN

> The whole house is on fire! We can't escape!

VLAD

> What time is it now, Sarah?

SARAH

> Almost eight.

VLAD

> American Idol is now on TV. Da?

SARAH

> Yes.

VLAD

> Let us all sit on couch like normal family.

MICHAEL

> Come on, Corin. Just sit on the couch and pretend like we're a normal family watching American Idol.

> *(They sit on the couch as the American Idol theme plays and the house burns. Lights fade.)*

END OF PLAY.

PROSPERO'S MACHINE

Characters

LITTLE GIRL
A young girl, Prospero's daughter

PROSPERO
Magician and salesman, 30s

TOM
A peasant, 30s

ANNE BOLEYN
Queen of England, 20s

MICHELLE
Lady-in-waiting to the Queen, 20s

KING HENRY THE EIGHTH
King of England, 40s

GUY
Henry's servant, 30s

AN ANGEL

A TRUMPETER

Setting

England in the sixteenth century.

ACT I, SCENE I

(In the darkness we hear a LITTLE GIRL'S VOICE.*)*

LITTLE GIRL'S VOICE
Daddy- was I asleep?

PROSPERO
Be a good little mouse, sweetie, and go back to sleep.

LITTLE GIRL'S VOICE
I can't sleep unless you tell me a story. Tell me the story about how Mommy was the Queen.

PROSPERO
Well, alright. I'll tell you that story one more time, but you have to promise you will go to sleep when I'm finished.

LITTLE GIRL'S VOICE
I promise.

PROSPERO
Well, as you know, your Daddy is a Wizard who has figured out the secret of the Philosopher's Stone, but before I had the Philosopher's Stone, I was an inventor and a salesman. Of course, things really changed for me the day I figured out the secret. I was no longer restricted by my physical state and I could visit any time or assume any shape- a house, a bird, a man, a mouse, a wizard, a lizard, a clown or a louse.

(We hear the LITTLE GIRL'S VOICE *laugh.)*

Now Sweetie, I want you to know how strange a dream can be- if you close your eyes, you will be able to see. Close your eyes, do you see me? First thing I did was take my luggage and my magical box to England in the sixteenth century...I had come to look for rare books, because as you know, your Daddy loves to collect books.

LITTLE GIRL'S VOICE
I know Daddy.

PROSPERO
I didn't expect to appear in front of anyone, but I did, I appeared in front of Tom... I didn't plan it this way, but as it happened, I did need someone to help me with all my luggage.

(Lights up -we see PROSPERO *struggling with four suitcases. There is a box on the ground in front of him. He turns and sees* TOM. *Both men are startled.)*

TOM
Ahhhhh!!!!!!

PROSPERO
Ahhhhh!!!!!

TOM
Oh my God. *(Falls to his knees.)* Are you a Wizard? Are you real?

PROSPERO
Please forgive me. I didn't mean to startle you. I am Prospero, a good Wizard, one who is holy and who seeks no harm but says only God be with you and your family, Sir.

TOM
A good Wizard? Have you appeared here to grant my wish?

PROSPERO
Oh, no. This is just a coincidence. I didn't plan to appear in front of anyone. I do apologize. *(He tries to lift his suitcases.)* I've come here

actually to look for rare books; you see I am a great lover of books... I don't know why I chose this century, sort of random really.

TOM

A true Wizard? You mean all the children's stories are true?

PROSPERO

Oh yes, yes indeed they are. Could you tell me where the nearest village is?

TOM

Well, it's through the valley around the river bend, that way.

PROSPERO

And what's this village called?

TOM

It's my village; we call it Riverhere.

PROSPERO

Such a quaint and simple folk! *(Trying to carry his suitcases.)*

TOM

May I help you carry your things Master?

PROSPERO

No need. I... *(Struggling.)* I seem to be able to carry everything except my magic box.

TOM

Magic box?

PROSPERO

Yes, that's what I call it. It's my most favourite invention. I'm hoping it will help me to acquire some rare and unusual books.

TOM

Master, I am afraid.

PROSPERO

Don't be afraid. No honestly, there is no need.*(He puts down his suit-cases and opens the box and takes out the Anodyne Foot Therapy System.)* May I ask you your name?

TOM

My name is Tom Strun.

PROSPERO

You see Tom, I am really just a salesman at heart, and this is the most incredible product of all time. It's the amazing new Anodyne Solar Powered Foot Therapy System.

TOM

My word, my Lord, this must be a sign from heaven!

PROSPERO

Would you like to try it?

TOM

No. Not me. I couldn't.

PROSPERO

No. You don't want to try it? Ok, well, that's fine. Nobody is forcing you.

TOM

Oh, but sir, it does seem I slip upon the path of destiny by refusing. I wish to overcome my fears. How does this strange object get its magic?

PROSPERO

You see, that's the best part. It gets its energy from the sun. It's the new Solar Powered Foot Therapy System from Anodyne! *(Flips the switch, we hear a mechanical hum and gurgling of water.)* You just flip the switch to start the whirlpool of warm Epsom salt water and the rotating foot pads will soothe the feet in precisely programmed ways. Say good-bye to sore aching feet. You see, Tom, foot therapy is the most incredible and effective therapy in the universe! The feet actually hold the key to the greatest mysteries – bet you didn't know that did you?

TOM

Foot therapy?

PROSPERO

You've got me started now, Tom. I do understand that you cannot possibly comprehend such subtleties as the Universal Love Force Energy™ and its relationship to the many meridians and analogous microcosms that exist within your feet. But Tom, just think for a moment about your feet. They ground you to the earth, you balance perfectly upon them, it is only man and woman that can stand upright, animals are given over to gravity and to satisfying the impulses of the purely physical. Man and woman alone can lift themselves upright and reach up and back to contemplate the stars above them. This also frees the hands to be put together, right and left, to contemplate polarities and through prayer to come into consciousness and a true understanding of good and evil.

TOM

Oh, my Lord and saviour, you are a prophet!

PROSPERO

Not at all, Sir. I am like you, Sir, or rather, was once just like you. It was through foot therapy that I changed my destiny, and through foot therapy, you too can change your destiny.

TOM

May I be your apprentice? Please, Master, teach me your secrets!

PROSPERO

No. This is not well.

TOM

But you understand, you have knowledge!

PROSPERO

Oh yes, but meaningless words to you my friend.

TOM

Oh my Master, please accept me as your humble servant!

PROSPERO

No, this is not well. This is an accident. I have nothing you can use.

TOM

(Beside himself.) Noooo!!!! Please! Please! Please! No danger is too much for the secret of power! Please! I want the secret of power! Please! Power! I, Tom Strun, do solemnly swear before God to serve you honestly and righteously- to protect you with my very life if necessary- as your humble servant.

PROSPERO

No.

TOM

Master, please teach me, I'll not meet another like you! I beg you, Master, please, to just give me a chance. I beg you, please Master. Please! Please!

PROSPERO

Oh dear. What have I gotten myself into?

TOM

I will carry all your bags, prepare your meals, wash your garments, just tell me whatever it is that you want and I will do it.

PROSPERO

You see, Tom; I'm here to look for rare books.

TOM

Books? There are not many books around here master, but it is said that Her Majesty Anne Boleyn is a great lover of books, and she is in the area today to attend a funeral!

PROSPERO

Anne Boleyn? Oh dear. What year is it?

TOM

Why it is the year of our Lord 1536 Master.

PROSPERO

Anne Boleyn?

TOM

Yes. Queen consort of the British Isles, yes, the new wife of King Henry Number Eight- I happen to know a woman whose cousin is the carpenter who fashioned the coffin for Anne Boleyn's goddaughter, who is the deceased, God rest her soul. The funeral is taking place here today –but it is a most private affair...I have discovered however that Her Majesty Anne Boleyn does enjoy going on private walks with her French servant and will be doing so tomorrow in a tranquil forest near the village- one I happen to know quite well because as it happens another cousin of mine is the Forester of this very forest- it would be a simple thing for us to have a surprise meeting with her- most likely tomorrow, Master.

PROSPERO

Interesting; and you say she is a lover of books?

TOM

Yes. It is well known that her Majesty reveres learning above all else.

PROSPERO

Well, that does seem like a good plan Tom.

TOM

Thank you Master! Thank you! Let me carry your things. Come with me, my home is humble master, but I will prepare you a meal, come with me and we can rest and tomorrow I will speak with my cousin. I guarantee he will help us. Please, Master, follow me.

PROSPERO

All right, Tom. All right, I do need your help carrying my belongings so let us go then.

(Exeunt.)

ACT I. SCENE II.

(It is night. Enter ANNE BOLEYN *and her French servant* MICHELLE. *They are both dressed in black.* MICHELLE *carries a lantern.)*

ANNE

Oh Michelle, this is such a lovely walk- but I seem to have a stone in my boot! Could you please help me remove it?

MICHELLE

Of course Madame, if you would be so pleased as to sit upon this fallen tree.

ANNE

(ANNE sits down.) I'm afraid the boot has many laces. I can't imagine how the stone got in there.

MICHELLE

Such a lovely gown, Madame. You look radiant to the heavens.

ANNE

Oh Michelle, my most faithful servant, ever the flatterer. Yes, it is a lovely gown, even though it is for such a sad occasion.

MICHELLE

God rest her soul, Madame.

ANNE

God rest her soul. Oh Michelle look, you can see the stars. They are so beautiful. Perhaps she is already living among angels in the heavens. Oh dear, so many laces. Thank you so much my dear Michelle.

MICHELLE

Your grace, service to you is from my very soul in love.

ANNE

Good Lady Michelle, what do you think of England?

MICHELLE

I prefer a more southern exposure Madame.

ANNE

Nonsense. It is perfectly charming.

MICHELLE

Do you know Madame how much this single gown would be worth in the underground market?

ANNE

I suppose you would know about such things Michelle.

MICHELLE

The gown is silk and the lining is gold lace, the fur is mink and the brocade is silver.

ANNE

And I will only wear this dress once.

MICHELLE

I must now pull the boot Madame.

ANNE

Of course.

MICHELLE

(MICHELLE *pulls the boot off and a stone drops out.)* There is the culprit. Now we must put the boot back on.

ANNE

Yes my dear. *(A pause while they struggle with the boot.)* Oh Michelle. Life is so short, we really must thank God for every day we are alive.

MICHELLE

Yes Madame; but it is also true that we must sometimes allow ourselves to take risk and do forbidden things.

ANNE

You sometimes say such forbidden things Michelle.

MICHELLE

The forbidden fruit, do you think you would have tried it?

ANNE

Oh Michelle- behave- please- we mustn't.

MICHELLE

I would try it, Madame, just as we are taking a risk by taking our walks together in the forest. Life is only lived properly when one takes a risk.

ANNE

Michelle- dear- sometimes you do go too far into forbidden territory.

MICHELLE

Forgive me my Queen. I am a fool. My darkest fear is to fall from your Majesty's grace, because of my deep, deep love for Your Majesty.

ANNE

Oh, Michelle, my most faithful servant.

MICHELLE

Your Majesty! *(She falls to the ground and kisses* ANNE'S *feet.)*

ANNE

Stop that nonsense. Rise, rise, you are forgiven.

MICHELLE

Madame. *(She rises, they both laugh.)* Isn't it so lovely in the forest at this hour? Look at the stars!

ANNE

They are so beautiful, but we really must be going, it is so late.

MICHELLE

Yes Madame, let us go.

(Exeunt.)

ACT I. SCENE III.

(Enter TOM *and* PROSPERO. PROSPERO *is winded from carrying the suitcases.)*

PROSPERO

Tom. May we stop a while and look at the stars?

TOM

*(*TOM *puts down the box.)* Yes Master, let us rest a little. *(Puts down the suitcases.)*

PROSPERO

Thank you so much for your help, how can I ever repay you?

TOM

*(*TOM *falls to his knees.)* By saying you will accept me as your apprentice and teach me some magic.

PROSPERO

Well, yes I can try. *(He sits down upon his magic box.)*

TOM

Really? Do you think I could become a Wizard?

PROSPERO

Yes. Anyone who studies and works hard enough can become a Wizard.

TOM

What?

PROSPERO

Really- it is that simple. It will take many years of dedication, you have to do a lot of reading and practicing, but yes, you too can become a Wizard.

TOM

But I cannot read at all, Master.

PROSPERO

Well, it's a bit of an uphill struggle from here then, isn't it! Tom, I can see it now, you will one day learn to read. You simply must learn to read, Tom, because reading is the only way to learn magic. Books are the most magical of objects. That is why they have been so often destroyed by tyrants. Do you know how often books have been destroyed Tom? The library of Alexandria, the greatest library in ancient times, first put to the torch by Julius Caesar, then again in the third century by Diocletian, and the final blow in the fifth century by Bishop Cyril- tens of thousands of ancient books destroyed. In the twelfth century when the crusaders captured Tripoli they burned over one hundred thousand books of Muslim learning- and again in the thirteenth century when the crusaders captured Constantinople, that was the single biggest loss of classical literature. Every time a book is burned something precious is lost forever. Of course I am here hoping particularly to find books in English. You really have got me going Tom, I must say, we should continue before I ramble on.

TOM

Of course, Master. Let us continue. It is not much farther.

PROSPERO

Yes, Tom, yes- show me the way.

TOM

It's this way, not much farther, Master, if you please, just to follow me.

(Exeunt.)

ACT 1. SCENE IV.

(ANNE enters her dressing chamber carrying a lantern. There is a partition.)

ANNE

Michelle, could you bring my night gown and come and help me with my corset?

MICHELLE

(MICHELLE enters.) Yes Madame.

ANNE

We simply must be back in London by the end of the week. Oh Michelle, I wish we could stay a little while longer.

MICHELLE

(As they speak MICHELLE unties ANNE'S corset and helps her undress.) As do I, Madame.

ANNE

Though I am Queen of England, I am no better than a prisoner in truth. Tell me more stories about Bohemia, Michelle.

MICHELLE

Bohemia, Madame. Well, there is a free principality in Bohemia, Madame, in Heidelberg- the Palatinate. It is a community of free thinkers where one can hide in plain sight among the free, away from the ignorance of arbitrary rules and regulations.

ANNE

It sounds perfectly marvellous. Of course being Henry's wife, I could never know such a place.

MICHELLE

It is unfortunate, Madame, because you are a heroine among them. They would love you as much as I love you.

ANNE

> I have heard it is one of the wonders of the world.

MICHELLE

> The view from the mountain is breath-taking Madame, and the castle grounds have a secret underground labyrinth, which can only be experienced, as words alone, truly, cannot describe it Madame. It is a place where the ancient mysteries are still very much alive. Ever since Martin Luther nailed his theses to the church door in Wittenberg many of the Germanic princes have formed an alliance with Schmalkalden to defend the reformation. Some have taken Luther's ideas even farther.

ANNE

> I have absolutely no reservations, Michelle. I know God is with us.

MICHELLE

> It is a place where many of the artists and thinkers have gathered. There are many musicians and there is always dancing and singing and drinking of ale. The castle is occupied by Ludwig the fifth and it is his daughter, Margaret La Petite-Pierre, she is the reason for the freedom of this principality. All subjects are discussed, even the ancient Egyptian ideas.

ANNE

> There are those in England who despise me Michelle, who have accused me of witchcraft because of what I have done. There are those who have said that I have six toes and that I am cursed with an evil curse. How I sometimes wish I could escape to Bohemia!

MICHELLE

> Perhaps we might leave in disguise so our absence would be unnoticed until we were quiet out of reach.

ANNE

> Oh, that does amuse me, Michelle, me in disguise!

MICHELLE

> What sort of disguise would please Madame?

ANNE

I should like to be disguised as a lovely white mouse. *(They laugh.)*

MICHELLE

How lovely and foolish a disguise! I'm sure it would work! Think of it Madame! I know you are a student of courtly love- and as such you appreciate song and are an accomplished musician.

ANNE

Nothing nurtures the soul more than song.

MICHELLE

Can you imagine, Madame, to sing freely until thy voice is but a whisper?

ANNE

Such pleasures are lost to me Michelle.

MICHELLE

Not so Madame; It could truly be possible for us to escape.

ANNE

Really Michelle, such impertinence! Pass me my night gown. *(She goes behind the partition to put on her night gown.)*

MICHELLE

Forgive me my Queen- it is only my love and adoration that allows me to entertain such forbidden obsessions. As I was saying before, this gown, it is worth a small fortune, Madame.

ANNE

What? Well, I suppose it is rather valuable.

MICHELLE

It is worth enough to secure your escape.

ANNE

Escape? From what shall I escape? Royalty? From Holy Matrimony? From my love, my King, my Kingdom?

MICHELLE

Honestly, Madame- your position is not so secure, your failure to produce a male heir...

ANNE

Whatever do you mean? You don't by any chance mean the axe and the axe-man do you?

MICHELLE

Well- Henry can be quite unpleasant Madame.

ANNE

You know, you really have gone too far this time.

MICHELLE

I don't care. Do I venture into forbidden territory? So be it! King Henry is unpleasant and sometimes dangerously unpleasant- you must admit this is true.

ANNE

He is perhaps not very sensitive, but I must remind you Michelle, that he is my husband, and the King of England besides!

MICHELLE

He can be dangerously mean. Plus, I have heard he is covered in the most unpleasant boils and soars.

ANNE

Well...

MICHELLE

So it's true?

ANNE

He is the King, Michelle.

MICHELLE

I am afraid of him Madame. I am afraid of him.

ANNE

> Stop it!

MICHELLE

> If we go back to London it will be too late!

ANNE

> Stop this nonsense at once Michelle. I'll have none of it. I mean it.

MICHELLE

> As you wish Madame. In that case, I will say good night.

ANNE

> *(ANNE emerges in her night gown. They embrace.)* I am leaving you now my dear, and no more talk of free thinkers and the underground, Michelle, is that clear?

MICHELLE

> Yes. Perfectly clear.

ANNE

> Goodnight my dear.

MICHELLE

> Goodnight my Queen.

> *(ANNE exits.)*

> As clear as mud.

> *(MICHELLE exits. Fade to black.)*

ACT I. SCENE V.

(Enter TOM *with a torch. He lights several lanterns.* PROSPERO *follows with his luggage.)*

TOM
> Please come into my home Master.

PROSPERO
> You live in a secluded little clearing by the river?

TOM
> It's not much. It's just a simple home.

PROSPERO
> It's very pleasant Tom. Have you lived here all your life?

TOM
> Well, no. First it was my sister and her cow that lived here. Then, when she married, my brother moved in and lived here, but he went off to war and never came back. Now it's just me who lives here, Master. Just me.

PROSPERO
> And what is your trade, Tom?

TOM
> My trade? Well, I grow turnips and cabbages in a field up the hill and I sell them when they are in season. In the winter I'm a farmhand in the neighbouring shire. The truth is, my life is lonely- I've not been lucky in love.

PROSPERO
> Ah yes, love. Finding love can be quite a challenge.

TOM
> Yes. It can be. Can I offer you some ale, Master?

PROSPERO

That would be splendid.

TOM

Coming right up! (TOM *goes and gets the ale gives a mug to* PROSPERO.)

PROSPERO

Thank you so much. (PROSPERO *takes a sip.*)

TOM

How is the ale Master?

PROSPERO

It is very good, very good indeed Tom.

TOM

Master, do you think you could maybe, possibly teach me some love magic? Magic that might fetch me a wife?

PROSPERO

I have only two words for you Tom. Foot. Therapy.

TOM

Foot therapy?

PROSPERO

Yes, Tom. Foot therapy is the most amazing and subtle art. Allow me to explain. Let me show you my foot Tom.

(PROSPERO *removes his footwear.*)

The feet are the key to tapping into the cosmic energy of the universe. It is very complex, but I will teach you a little something. Listen carefully and you will learn. In your foot on average there are twenty-six small bones. In the toes, fourteen phalanges- above that, five metatarsal bones- above that, three cuneiform bones- above that, here, is the navicular and here the cuboid- the heel is the calcaneous bone- and above that connecting us to our ankles we have the talus. These are joined together with connective tissue, blood vessels and nerves and covered in a layer of skin. This finely tuned structure is balanced on two main arches- one from the heel to the base of the little toe, the other from the heel to the big toe. Now listen carefully Tom, if we are looking at the body from directly the front, or the back for that matter, each toe draws a meridian straight up the body all the way to the head, creating ten areas that cover the entire body.

TOM

I think I understand, Master.

PROSPERO

These are just the longitudinal zones Tom, there are many others; these ones are, however, the easiest to understand.

TOM

Oh Master, thank you for teaching me this wonderful medicine.

PROSPERO

Now listen, Tom- although it is vastly more complex than this- but here in the soft area of the arches, one can treat all the internal organs through massage. Here is the liver, here the gall bladder, here the stomach, the pancreas, duodenum, spleen, kidneys, adrenals- but I want you to remember just one Tom and it is here. This is the area on a woman's foot that stimulates her...(*Makes a whistling sound- an ascending and descending note that match the syllables for hel-lo.*)

TOM

Oh Master, I am not worthy of this.

PROSPERO

Nonsense Tom. Do me a favour and take off your shoes. (*PROSPERO gets up and removes the Solar Powered Footbath from its box.*)

TOM

Take off my shoes?

PROSPERO

Come on, don't be shy!

TOM

> I almost never take off my shoes, Master. I sometimes even sleep in them.

PROSPERO

> You don't!

TOM

> Yes I do.

PROSPERO

> Well that's simply got to stop. Come on now. Take these shoes off.

> (TOM *removes his footwear and his feet are very dirty.* PROSPERO *flips the switch and turns on his machine.*)

> Oh dear, Tom, you've really got to take better care of your feet. First, let's get these feet into ship-shape by putting them into the new Anodyne Solar Powered Foot Therapy System, an Anodyne product under the Anodyne trademark. Come on Tom, in they go.

TOM

> (TOM *puts his feet into the machine.*) Oh what a lovely sensation!

PROSPERO

> Now all we're going to do is add a little tea tree oil to the water. There we go- the tea tree oil comes as a special added bonus.

TOM

> What a magical odour Master, sweet and pleasant like no scent I've ever known!

PROSPERO

> Now then, don't be afraid, Tom, but I am going to wash your feet in the special Anodyne soap and water combination. I think you'll agree it's the most pleasant, most agreeable sensation you've ever had or your money back. *(Takes* TOM'S *foot.)* Now pay close attention Tom, this is the area on a woman's foot I want you to remember.

TOM

No Master- no. I don't deserve this knowledge- what are you doing!

PROSPERO

I'm stimulating your mind in such a way that emotional issues are coming up for you.

TOM

You're right Master- I can't bear it! *(Buries his face in his hands.)*

PROSPERO

Now Tom, this is only the beginning, the feet are one of the places you store all your emotions, they are the locus of your vulnerability.

TOM

(Crying.) Yes Master, you are absolutely right.

PROSPERO

There, there, little man.

TOM

Oh! Whaaaaa!

PROSPERO

That's it Tom, let it all out.

TOM

I'm nothing. I'm a nobody!

PROSPERO

That's not true!

TOM

Yes Master. I'm not worthy to worship at your feet!

PROSPERO

You see! There it is! There it is embedded in your language- in the very vernacular with which you express yourself. You see- already you've imbued the feet with notions of submission and domination. There in lies a sure sign of your lack of emotional health. Your feet should be free Tom- your feet should be your friends.

TOM

My feet, my lord, my...friends?

PROSPERO

Yes! Free your feet, Tom!

TOM

Master- may I please put my shoes back on?

PROSPERO

Well. I'm not going to stop you- but- listen, Tom, I am a Wizard. I do know a thing or two. You must trust me. Go barefoot Tom. Give your feet some breathing room- you can't go around stuffing them into stinky, sordid footwear all the time. You've got to free them! Doesn't it feel good?

TOM

(Crying.) Yes- it feels good!

PROSPERO

Then why are you crying?

TOM

Because I'm nothing! I'm nobody. *(Panicking.)* And my feet are filthy. Lord!

PROSPERO

Don't you see? They're not! Not since you put them in the new Anodyne Solar Powered Foot Therapy System they're not! Now they're relaxed and pleasant smelling!

TOM

Yes! Yes! They are. But they're still filthy! Because I'm filthy! *(Puts his footwear back on.)*

PROSPERO

You see- it's only in your head. You've got nice feet Tom.

TOM
What?

PROSPERO
Yes. You heard me right. You've got nice feet.

TOM
I don't believe this. Nothing ever happens to me. My life has been dull -dull -dull. I've been waiting all my life for love but all it's ever been is turnips and cabbages. I wake up, tend the fields, harvest turnips and cabbages, tidy the hut; sit by the river, eat turnips and cabbages and drink ale. All the women I know are married and I'm all alone, and all I have are my turnips and cabbages. I'm a failure- a turnip and cabbage failure.

PROSPERO
Well, trust me Tom, become a student of foot therapy and you will unleash the Universal Love Force Energy™. I know it seems farfetched to you- perhaps impossible- but you must have faith in the Anodyne Corporation and the new Anodyne Solar Powered Foot Therapy System. Your life can change Tom- it will change.

TOM
(With sudden alacrity.) Yes! It will change! Yes!

PROSPERO
That's the spirit! Yes!

TOM
(With sudden despondence.) Oh Master. But I have such loneliness- such deep and painful yearnings.

PROSPERO
Tut tut! Listen to me Tom- let's sleep now, we have a big day tomorrow. But I want you to free your feet Tom. Tonight, remove your shoes before you go to bed.

TOM
Remove my shoes?

PROSPERO

Yes Tom- go to bed barefoot. You simply must.

TOM

All right Master, all right. I will. If you say I must, then I will, Master.

PROSPERO

That's it. Good man- now- off to bed. Tomorrow is a big day and I want us to be well rested.

TOM

Yes. Master, come with me. I'll show you where you will be sleeping.

PROSPERO

Yes Tom. Yes. You show me.

TOM

Just come this way.

(Exeunt.)

ACT I. SCENE VI.

(Enter KING HENRY NUMBER EIGHT*; he is in a chamber in the Tower of London.)*

HENRY

> Servant! Where in Heaven's name are you? Present yourself!

GUY

> *(Enter* GUY, *his servant.)* I'm here your Majesty! I'm right here.

HENRY

> Come here, servant. *(*GUY *approaches* HENRY.*)* You have made us wait. *(*HENRY *proceeds to flick him in the nose.)*

GUY

> Ouch!

HENRY

> My word, Servant, your nose really is big and red and swollen, isn't it? *(He flicks him again.)*

GUY

> Ohhhhh! Yes, Your Majesty. It is.

HENRY

> You shall observe, servant, as thoughts come forth from the fount of our most divine wisdom.

GUY

> Yes, your highest munificence, most glorious Majesty.

HENRY

> Much better; you are a good servant after all. We contemplate upon polygamy, servant, and we see it is not the Christian way, but more the way of the Saracen infidel. We shall suffer not the Saracen heresy. Rather, we most emphatically praise the author of "A Glasse of the Truthe." A most sound work.

GUY

Indeed, your greatness, a most profound work of political philosophy. *(Aside.)* In truth, it's a book that he wrote.

HENRY

We believe the Salic law regarding male inheritance to be proper.

GUY

Oh yes. The Frankish kings know how to live.

HENRY

The realm must have princes- male heirs. For no realm should be ruled by a female.

GUY

Yes. Princes. *(HENRY flicks him in the nose again.)* Ohhhhhh!

HENRY

We have a job for you, servant. You are to spy on Her Ladyship Anne Boleyn. Tell us who her adulterous companions are. Return successfully and we will see to it that you are not punished for the naming of names.

GUY

Names? *(HENRY flicks Guy in the nose.)* Ohhh. Ohhhh. Yes, Your Munificent Majesty. The wisdom of God spews forth from the font of light that is your radiance.

HENRY

You are a good subject after all. Now go!

(Exeunt.)

ACT II. SCENE I.

(It is daytime in the forest. TOM *enters.)*

TOM

> Oh, I told my Master to meet me here- and I fear he has abandoned me. Everything has gone so well with my cousin the Forester, and Her Majesty the Queen will be coming this way soon. I made sure my Master knew the exact spot, but I fear I have lost him! I am afraid he has changed his mind and he has left the village. I don't blame him. Why would anyone put their trust in me? What am I doing? This is dangerous! What was I thinking? No matter what I do -it never works out! I'm so stupid. Master? Master? Where are you? We spent so much time this morning rehearsing our presentation and now this, I lose my Master!

PROSPERO

> *(Offstage.)* Tom!

TOM

> Master! Is it you?

PROSPERO

> *(*PROSPERO *enters with twelve books in his arms.)* Look at this treasure I've discovered! Twelve of them! Twelve being a very important number- as you will someday see Tom, a very musical number!

TOM

> But where did you find them?

PROSPERO

> You won't believe it. They were in the garbage, in a ditch just outside the chapel wall! They are filthy, but we can clean them. Can you believe our luck? Look at these titles! These two are not in English- French Recipes and Rhymes- and The Lover and the Beloved in Catalan by Ramon Lull! But they are magnificent! And the rest are all Farmers' Almanacs, all in English Tom. I couldn't believe my lucky stars, I was

just walking along and I saw them in the ditch just rotting away! I scooped them up, wiped them off and now they will be part of my library! Here, take these and keep them safe!

TOM

Yes Master, but now we must hide in the bushes and wait. Her Majesty Anne Boleyn will be along any minute. Hurry, here they come Master, hurry, we must hide ourselves!

(They hide. The audience can still see them as ANNE *and* MICHELLE *enter.)*

MICHELLE

My Lady, you are gifted with qualities rarely found even in the noblest of men.

ANNE

There are those who say that Fortune hates Virtue- but I don't agree. Indeed, in all of us there is a seed of folly which, if left unchecked will grow indefinitely- and it is this seed that we must vigilantly and virtuously resist by the pursuit of knowledge, talent, good looks and disposition- and of grace, which makes a person always pleasing at first sight.

TOM

(Whispers.) This is the perfect time for us to present ourselves, Master.

PROSPERO

Patience, Tom- I want to listen to our Lady and hear what she has to say. I had no idea how beautiful she is!

MICHELLE

Oh Madame, my Queen- I am most moved by your eloquence.

ANNE

Virtue, Michelle. That is the quality God desires of his children, and for which Fortune changes her course. Virtue through self-improvement, resilience and spirit- not merely day by day, but with an infinite range, Michelle.

MICHELLE
And these, as you say, are the true skills of the courtier?

ANNE
Yes. Michelle. These skills are the secret wealth of the soul, taken notice of by both heavenly and earthly Kings and Queens. Fortune may improve its course for one with the proper application of discipline and self improvement.

MICHELLE
As it has for you Madame?

ANNE
Yes Michelle. Let us stop here for a rest. I should like to relate some of my experience. Michelle, those who behave with grace will find it in others. Some say that grace is a natural gift, but I say it is not so. It can be greatly enhanced by application and effort. And remember this most of all, Michelle: practice in all things a certain nonchalance and humility which conceals all artistry and makes whatever one says or does seem effortless and uncontrived.

PROSPERO
(PROSPERO *emerges from the bushes.*) Please excuse our rudeness Your Majesty, allow me to make my introduction.

MICHELLE
(MICHELLE *draws a dagger.*) Stand back if you value your life!

TOM
(TOM *pops out of the bushes.*) Do not threaten my Master!

MICHELLE
Who is this? Peasant! I'll dispatch you presently!

TOM
You?

ANNE
Stop, Michelle.

PROSPERO

My Lady- it is my firm wish to please- Your Majesty- I kneel before you. I come a humble servant to Your Majesty.

MICHELLE

Don't listen to him, Madame!

ANNE

Nonsense Michelle. You may present yourself sir.

PROSPERO

I am none other than Prospero, Your Majesty- salesman and Wizard.

MICHELLE

Wizard? Ridiculous Madame, and salesman! Ha!

TOM

Do not laugh at my Master.

MICHELLE

You, sir, are in grave danger.

ANNE

Remember grace and good manners Michelle- these gentlemen are my subjects and it is my pleasure to indulge them.

MICHELLE

Really Madame? A Wizard? Nonsense!

ANNE

Michelle, desist.

MICHELLE

As you wish, Madame.

ANNE

Prospero?

PROSPERO

At your service, Your Majesty.

ANNE

An odd name for an odd looking gentleman.

PROSPERO

I have come to introduce to you, Your Majesty, the most remarkable product of all time.

MICHELLE

Don't listen Madame- he's a man of no means- his only offering is bread crust!

TOM

Speak not of my lord thus!

MICHELLE

Speak not at all Lord Lad! Madame, do not trust these men.

ANNE

Enough, Michelle!

PROSPERO

Your Majesty- please, let me first say that you are the wisest of all ladies. Your understanding of good manners, learning, music and art have made me- a Wizard- revere your opinions above all others. I wish to introduce to you a device that for you, more than any other human being, will bring satisfaction. Your Majesty, I introduce to you: the new Anodyne Solar Powered Foot Therapy System. Tom- as we rehearsed it.

TOM

Yes Master. It's the new Solar Powered Foot Therapy System from Anodyne- just press this button to start the whirlpool of warm, Epsom salt water, and the patented rotating foot pads will sooth the feet in precisely programmed ways. Say goodbye to sore, aching feet. Foot therapy is the most amazing medicine known to science. You'll feel better than ever before, and all your problems will magically disappear. It's really amazing! Just find a comfortable place to sit, cast in thy feet and enjoy the pleasant, relaxing sensation.

ANNE
A footbath?

PROSPERO
Yes, Your Majesty. A solar-powered footbath! Can you think of anything more enlightened?

ANNE
Solar Powered?

TOM
Examine if you will, Exhibit A: my foot.

PROSPERO
The feet are a microcosm of the universe, Your Majesty- over twenty-six separate bones and many meridians make the feet a veritable conduit for the Universal Love Force Energy™.

TOM
I used to be nothing but a turnip and cabbage failure- but when I started foot therapy, I changed my destiny. You too can change your destiny with the miracle of foot therapy.

PROSPERO
We, all of us, take our feet for granted. We stand upon them, balance perfectly upon them, dance upon them- they ground us to the earth, our planet- and we all walk around as though it were nothing special, pretending that we understood this miracle known as the foot. It is only man and woman that can stand upright, animals are given over to gravity and to satisfying the impulses of the purely physical. Man and woman alone can lift themselves upright and reach up and back to contemplate the stars above them. This also frees the hands to be put together, right and left, to contemplate polarities and through prayer to come into consciousness and a true understanding of good and evil. Do you ever wonder why we have ten toes, not eight or four or two? The number ten, as Pythagoras shows, is the perfect number- reducing to the one, also the octave, as well as the perfect harmonies in the major scale all at once.

ANNE

>Ah, yes. I am familiar with these Pythagorean principals, and I am happy to say that I do have ten toes.

PROSPERO

>You are? *(Pause.)* Yes, you are. And this is why of all endorsements, yours is worth the most. Of all Ladies of all time- it is you, Anne Boleyn, who deserves to change her destiny.

ANNE

>My destiny? *(She holds her neck.)* I suddenly feel strange. Continue on Prospero. I have an intuition that you perhaps are a true wizard.

TOM

>He is a true wizard, Your Majesty!

MICHELLE

>*(Laughing.)* What nonsense!

TOM

>Don't talk to me like that!

MICHELLE

>You, sir, are a scurrilous, foolish ass.

TOM

>Well you, Madame, are a he goat.

MICHELLE

>Words cannot express the degrees to which I revile thee, Monsieur!

ANNE

>Enough, Michelle. Desist, both of you. Carry on, Prospero. You have my attention.

PROSPERO

>After years of studying the foot -the Anodyne Corporation has designed a solar-powered footbath that offers the most pleasant, most relaxing sensation of your life time.

TOM

To order the Anodyne Foot Therapy System just dial the number on the screen. Don't delay! The Anodyne Corporation: we have all the answers.

ANNE

What number screen?

PROSPERO

Don't worry about that part Majesty- that is for the future. *(He winks at the audience.)* After a long hard day of walking upon feet bound and misshapen into what can only be called cruel and unusual foot-wear, what could be more soothing than a relaxing and therapeutic foot bath?

TOM

But is this product safe?

PROSPERO

Why, yes Tom! This product is as safe as milk. There are absolutely no negative side effects. The positive effects of foot therapy are, however, too numerous to count! It's really that amazing.

TOM

Do I need any special accessories, Master?

PROSPERO

That's the best part Tom! The Anodyne Foot Therapy System is solar powered, all you need to do is leave it in the sun and you will have all the energy you need to heat the water and power the rotating foot pads.

TOM

It's really just amazing.

PROSPERO

And that's not all! As an added bonus we include tea tree oil and our special Anodyne bar of soap! So with each treatment we can wash and perfume the feet at the same time as treating them therapeutically.

TOM

That really is amazing!

PROSPERO

> You get the tea tree oil treatment with the bar of soap and a session with the footbath and all I ask in payment are books- I am a mad collector of books.

MICHELLE

> Madame, these men are highway bandits!

PROSPERO

> Of course I wouldn't suggest that Your Majesty use my service without first trying it out for free.

MICHELLE

> Do you mean to suggest that Her Majesty remove her footwear!

PROSPERO

> To free her feet? I most emphatically do. Yes. For more than any other woman of all time, she should be pampered- she has worked so hard to be pleasant, learned and graceful.

ANNE

> I would like to try it! Michelle, help me remove my shoes.

MICHELLE

> Madame, you would expose the Royal feet?

ANNE

> The Royal feet, toes and ankles.

TOM

> Ankles too?

MICHELLE

> As you wish Madame. *(Removes* ANNE'S *shoes.)*

PROSPERO

> Your Majesty! *(Bows.)* Witness the beauty and elegance of this most royal foot.

MICHELLE
You are not worthy of such a sight, sir.

TOM
(TOM *falls to his knees and lowers his head.*) Master, such beautiful dainty little feet she has.

PROSPERO
Yes, she does. Come over here, Your Majesty. Sit upon this fallen tree and let us admire the mystery of the universe. (ANNE *holds out her foot.*) Such lovely examples of naked perfection.

ANNE
You're too kind.

PROSPERO
First, allow me to add the tea tree oil to the water. If it pleases Your Majesty that she might sample the fragrance?

ANNE
It smells wonderful. Such a scent I have never encountered. So lovely and unusual!

PROSPERO
Now cast in thy feet. Don't be shy.

ANNE
(*She puts her feet into the machine.*) Oh- lovely! Yes, most excellent.

PROSPERO
I think you'll agree, it is the most pleasant, most relaxing sensation of your lifetime.

ANNE
Oh, it is. It definitely is.

PROSPERO
Now, Your Majesty, I'll apply the special Anodyne soap and water combination. If you'll just let me therapeutically treat the Royal foot.

MICHELLE

(MICHELLE *draws her dagger.*) You would dare touch the Royal foot!

ANNE

Michelle, relax. Just you go over with Tom there and leave me and Prospero alone for a bit.

MICHELLE

Madame!

ANNE

You heard me!

MICHELLE

As you wish.

(TOM *and* MICHELLE *go off to one side while* PROSPERO *massages* ANNE'S *feet.* MICHELLE *grabs* TOM *by the collar.*)

MICHELLE

(Whispers.) I warn you, sir. You may have Her Majesty fooled but you have not fooled me.

TOM

We are not fooling anyone, Michelle. The Anodyne Solar Powered Foot Therapy System really is something amazing.

MICHELLE

Peasant. If you should harm a single hair on my Madame's head, I shall personally kill you. Do you understand?

TOM

Don't harm a hair or you'll kill me. Yes. Right. Got that. Clear and simple. (She lets go.) My word, you are a rough woman- do you treat your husband this way?

MICHELLE

Husband. Puh! I have no husband and answer to no man.

TOM

You have no husband?

MICHELLE

No. I have never met a man that didn't disgust me, sir.

TOM

Right.

MICHELLE

Men are the mortal enemies of all women. Like, for example, Her Majesty, who is in mortal danger- though she refuses to see it. Listen to me, sir. You tell your Master this: If he really loves my Madame he would help me organize her escape to the Palatinate Palace in Bohemia.

TOM

Palatinate Palace in Bohemia?

MICHELLE

That, sir, is a free principality where one can escape the ignorance and stupidity of regular rules and regulations.

TOM

Right.

MICHELLE

Tell your Master this: Her Majesty Anne Boleyn has fallen from the King's favor- she has failed to provide a male heir- and though His Majesty, King Henry Number Eight, seems to accept the young princess Elizabeth- my Madame's only daughter, it is only because he privately hopes to marry her off to a suitor that suits his own self-interest. However, he reviles my poor Madame and has developed an illicit, unhealthy and most dangerous obsession with Jane Seymour, a lady-in-waiting not unlike the lady-in-waiting that Madame Anne Boleyn once was. Presently, the King looks for any excuse to dispose of my Madame in order to have Jane Seymour as his bride. I for one, sir, am willing to lay down my life to save Her Majesty, a woman so virtuous she cannot see the evil nature of her own husband. You tell your master this. That if he is willing to help me, we may work together. And if not, then he must disappear, or face grave consequences. Do you understand that?

TOM
Right.

MICHELLE
Right.

PROSPERO
Tom?

TOM
Yes Master!

ANNE
What are you two whispering about, Michelle?

MICHELLE
Just that we should make our way home soon, Madame- before the weather turns.

ANNE
Yes indeed.

PROSPERO
Before you depart, may I ask Your Majesty's opinion of this wondrous machine?

ANNE
It is most excellent sir.

PROSPERO
Does Your Majesty wish to know more?

ANNE
Yes. Meet us again tomorrow in the town square. We journey back to London tomorrow. If you join us, we can make further arrangements. I do have one request, however. You say you are a Wizard, would you show me a magic trick?

PROSPERO

Why yes, Your Majesty! Of course! Do you see this kerchief? Examine it from front to back, from side to side- from zenith to nadir. Now watch closely as I stuff it into my hand. And now I open my hand and- presto! The kerchief is gone. Look at my hands- where can the kerchief be?

ANNE

Most amazing!

PROSPERO

Now, watch me make a fist and- presto! The kerchief is back!

MICHELLE

A mere parlor trick.

ANNE

Remember your manners, Michelle. That was a perfectly marvelous trick. I believe you are a true Wizard. Please take this little book as a present from me.

PROSPERO

Your Majesty, I am a great lover of books. I cannot thank you enough!

ANNE

Adieu, sir. Until we meet again tomorrow.

PROSPERO

Adieu, Your Majesty- to have an audience with you fulfills my life's ambition. Until we meet again. *(Bows.)*

ANNE

Farewell. *(ANNE and MICHELLE exit.)*

TOM

Master.

PROSPERO

Speak not to me just presently Tom as my entire being is radiating love for Her Majesty.

TOM

    I see. *(A beat.)* Master, may I speak now?

PROSPERO

    Yes Tom, yes.

TOM

    Master, Her Majesty Anne Boleyn's servant Michelle was very serious in her insistence that Her Majesty is in grave danger from his Royal Highness King Henry Number Eight.

PROSPERO

    Oh yes, I know all about that.

TOM

    You know? But how do you know that?

PROSPERO

    Because I am from the future Tom. I know the whole sad story. Her Majesty Anne Boleyn, who - after an epic struggle with the Church, replaced Catherine of Aragon as wife of Henry Number Eight, is herself beheaded by a special swordsman brought up to Tower Hill from Calais. On May 19th, 1536, Anne Boleyn is beheaded and eleven days later Henry is betrothed to Jane Seymour.

TOM

    May 19? Why, today is May 17! Is there anything we can do to stop this from happening Master?

PROSPERO

    I don't know.

TOM

    You don't know? But, Master! Michelle was very insistent that we either help her help Her Majesty escape to Bohemia or, she says- she'll kill us.

PROSPERO

    Well, we'll do what we can, but I don't know how or what or where anything can be done. Do you think one can change destiny, Tom?

TOM
    What, me? I don't know.

PROSPERO
    Perhaps some of us change our destinies and some of us don't.
    Perhaps the rules that apply to me don't apply to you; all laws are
    ultimately formless. Can we change destiny? I don't know- but I'll
    tell you one thing: if there is anyone who deserves a relaxing foot
    massage, it's her Majesty Anne Boleyn.

    (Exeunt.)

ACT 2. SCENE 2.

*(*MICHELLE *enters Anne's room.* ANNE *is seated at her vanity.)*

MICHELLE
    Madame?

ANNE
    Yes Michelle?

MICHELLE
    May I have a word with you?

ANNE
    You've been quiet this evening, unlike your usual mischievous self.
    What troubles you?

MICHELLE
    Madame- may I speak plainly?

ANNE
>   Plainly?

MICHELLE
>   Madame- for most people it is wise to hide our true feelings behind a
>   curtain of manners, but sometimes this can work against us. You are
>   a perceptive woman and you know that self-interest and ambition is
>   most often behind sweet words and adulations.

ANNE
>   Michelle. What are you trying to communicate?

MICHELLE
>   Madame- I have a most unsettling intuition. We cannot return to
>   London- it would be a grave mistake.

ANNE
>   Cannot?

MICHELLE
>   Madame. Excuse my forwardness. I am willing, as I've already made
>   clear to you, to risk my life for you... and the time has come to do away
>   with pretence and to make clear to you what you refuse to see.

ANNE
>   I am devoted to my husband, to my King. He is a wise and divine
>   sovereign and it is my duty as Queen of England and as a wife to be
>   obedient and devoted.

MICHELLE
>   Madame- everyone knows that he has turned his heart against you!

ANNE
>   Michelle, you are now out of your place and position.

MICHELLE
>   I don't care.

ANNE
>   You don't care?

MICHELLE

> Everyone knows that he feels you are cursed with an evil curse.

ANNE

> Enough!

MICHELLE

> Madame. I have nothing left to lose, and I say this from the depth of my soul. I admire you beyond any other person.

ANNE

> I am devoted to my King. I would give my life to him.

MICHELLE

> Yes. You would, but would you let him take a new wife?

ANNE

> What a monstrous suggestion!

MICHELLE

> Jane Seymour.

ANNE

> No.

MICHELLE

> Yes.

ANNE

> No.

MICHELLE

> Jane Seymour is the King's current obsession- just as you once were.

ANNE

> Enough!

MICHELLE

> He seeks a way to be rid of you, and he will stop at nothing, Madame. He is not afraid of doing whatever it takes to get his way.

ANNE

> There's nothing we can do. There is no answer.

MICHELLE

> There are often ways and means that escape attention by being too obvious.

ANNE

> What do you mean?

MICHELLE

> We could disguise ourselves- sell your gown and make our escape to Bohemia! The gown, piece by piece, could fetch enough money to survive for several years.

ANNE

> Do you think he couldn't find us there? Of course he could- he could find us anywhere. I must embrace my destiny, not run from it.

MICHELLE

> Madame, if we return to London it will be too late.

ANNE

> We shall return to London and we cannot talk of this ever again. No argument- I will do what my sovereign desires, and that includes giving my life. For King and country, Michelle, I would give my blood. Blood means nothing when weighed fairly with England. Honor and virtue are to me more important than escape- do you understand?

MICHELLE

> It is a sad and pitiful world that allows a cruel sovereign to abuse so noble a lady.

ANNE

> All will be well. Now remove that unpleasant frown from my presence. Go off to bed.

MICHELLE

> Madame, you are such a rare creature. The King has no sense.

ANNE

> Enough!

MICHELLE

> The King is vile. He is a vile and evil human being! I hate him! And I love you, Anne Boleyn. *(Curtsies, bowing her head.)* My Lady.

ANNE

> Michelle! You must never- do you hear me? Never speak in this manner again! I will not abide by it. You have used up your familiarity with me! You have transgressed for the last time!

MICHELLE

> Madame. Please, no!

ANNE

> Yes! To say this of your King is to say this of England! All that I have done- the break with Rome, the fight to be Queen- I have done all this for England. I would die for my King so that England could be born. You have misunderstood me, Michelle, you have misread me, and you have disappointed me.

MICHELLE

> Madame! Madame! *(Falls to her knees.)* Please forgive me!

ANNE

> I will not tolerate such disobedience from this point forward. Your lack of respect for your King is most ungracious Michelle and you have lost our trust and our respect. Good night! *(ANNE exits, leaving MICHELLE alone.)*

ACT 2. SCENE 3.

(PROSPERO *is sitting reading.* TOM *joins him.*)

TOM
> Master, is this the new book Her Majesty gave you?

PROSPERO
> Yes Tom.

TOM
> You wish to read it before you go to bed, Master?

PROSPERO
> Yes Tom. You have no idea what sort of book this is- most rare indeed. It's an old English translation of 'The Picatrix'- a truly magical book- a very rare find. It's a most ancient work translated from the Arabian tongue -and this one contains a unique commentary by the translator.

TOM
> Master, teach me some magic.

PROSPERO
> Your imagination is magic, Tom. You must think upon the miracle of your own imagination.

TOM
> Yes, Master. *(Pause.)* I don't know what you mean.

PROSPERO
> Tom, your imagination is magic, it is where things come into being. There is more to imagination than you might expect, it is very powerful. Writing and reading is truly magical. Look at these symbols- these books. Reading and writing is what makes you into a Wizard- one who can defy time and space.

TOM

I fear I shall never read or write particularly well, Master. I have tried to learn.

PROSPERO

Never use the word try Tom. You will learn to read because books are the most powerful of all things. Look at this little book, Tom. Isn't it beautiful? The leather binding, the gold lettering and illustrations- in this book live the ancient temples of Egyptian priests of the temple of the Sun. It contains the science and philosophy of an ancient writer- a Magi long, long, long since dead- and yet he lives! Is that not magical?

TOM

You mean he lives inside the book?

PROSPERO

Yes! There he is! You can see him in his words- his thoughts, his feelings.

TOM

Master. I cannot see him. (TOM *takes the book and looks inside.*)

PROSPERO

Yes. But if you read the book, you can! You will learn to read Tom. This is the Anodyne Corporation's whole premise- the premise of the Anodyne Foot Therapy System, an Anodyne product under the Anodyne trade mark. Can you change your destiny, Tom? We say, yes! Just purchase one of our Anodyne Foot Therapy System's Solar Powered Footbaths and yes- your life will change, for the better.

TOM

I wish I could purchase one, sir, but I have only this one coin, one coin in the whole world. *(Pause.)* Master, I would like to give it you. *(Gives* PROSPERO *his coin.)*

PROSPERO

Yes, well, money is essential Tom. I am imagining myself finding some rare books in the market tomorrow, so I will take this coin Tom. Money is a metaphysical phenomenon which I have found no way to escape from. You don't pay, you don't play, Tom. That's one of the first things you have to come to terms with. You need to come up with the money before you can really change your destiny.

TOM

Yes. I can see how that would be the case.

PROSPERO

It is possible Tom. You just have to use your imagination. I mean really use your imagination.

TOM

Yes. *(Pause.)* Oh Master. I am nothing but a country fool!

PROSPERO

Nonsense. You are a student therapist and an apprentice Wizard!

TOM

I am?

PROSPERO

You're more than a peasant, Tom. You're more than just dust in the wind.

TOM

I am?

PROSPERO

Yes. You're a foot specialist, and you should be proud!

TOM

That's right. I am! I am! I'm a foot specialist! *(Removes his shoes.)*

PROSPERO

Good man! Now, off to bed. We've got to be in top form tomorrow.

TOM

Yes Master. Good night!

PROSPERO

Good night! *(They go to bed.)*

ACT 3. SCENE 1.

(It is now daytime. TOM *waits in the town square.* PROSPERO *enters with four books in his hands.)*

PROSPERO
Tom. You will not believe this. Look what I have found!

TOM
Where did you find these ones?

PROSPERO
In a market stall! There was a man there who was passing through who said he had rare books, and I used the coin you gave me to purchase these books from him. Look at these titles! You won't believe this Tom, this is a collection of the lost books of Geoffrey Chaucer! "Of the Wreched Engendrynge of Mankynde," "Origenes upon the Maudeleyne," and "The book of the Leoun". Tom, I know you don't know who Chaucer is, but he is one of the greatest writers, "The Millers Tale", oh goodness gracious, who doesn't love Chaucer! Amazing find, this one! And this one, Secretum Secretorum, the lost treatise on immortality by Aristotle! These are exactly the kind of books I hoping for! I am just beside myself with joy Tom! This is the power of positive thinking Tom. Keep these safe. They are worth more than just money.

TOM
Yes Master.

PROSPERO
Now we wait here in the market square for the most virtuous of all creatures- who knows what strange forces she may inspire? What plans does the architect of our fate have in store for us today? Let me ask you- was it your fate to have become my student?

TOM
I suppose it was, Master, seeing as I am.

PROSPERO

What if I was to tell you that you don't exist- that you are a figment of the imagination. You are a trick; a brief candle.

TOM

I am not a trick to myself, Master.

PROSPERO

We are just poor players Tom- that strut and fret their hour upon this stage! *(Enter* ANNE *and* MICHELLE*)*

ANNE

Prospero. Today we shall once more discuss your most excellent foot-bath.

PROSPERO

My most gracious Lady, I am at your eternal service. *(He kneels.)*

ANNE

Prospero tell me, are you married?

PROSPERO

No, Your Majesty- I am married to my work. It is the Anodyne Corporation that gives my life meaning. It is the amazing Anodyne Solar Powered Foot Therapy System and the new Anodyne Solar Powered Footbath that fulfills my destiny and gives me the power to have crazy feet, Your Majesty.

ANNE

Crazy feet?

PROSPERO

(Whispers.) You do have crazy feet by the way.

ANNE

What do you mean?

PROSPERO

I say this from the place that I mean it most. You have beautiful feet.

ANNE
>   Oh Prospero. I feel overcome with a sudden darkness and sadness.

PROSPERO
>   Why?

ANNE
>   I don't know.

PROSPERO
>   I do.

ANNE
>   Why?

PROSPERO
>   Because you need a foot massage!

ANNE
>   You're right! But what about Henry?

PROSPERO
>   He needs a foot massage too, Your Majesty!

ANNE
>   His feet do ail him.

PROSPERO
>   Well, this Solar Powered Footbath is just what he needs.

ANNE
>   Yes. It truly is!

PROSPERO
>   Would my Lady care to remove her footwear so that she may enjoy, once again, the new Anodyne Solar Powered Foot Therapy System?

ANNE
>   Michelle, Tom- leave Prospero and I alone for a while.

MICHELLE
  Madame. *(Bows and they exit.)*

PROSPERO
  Are you listless? Do you find it difficult to achieve total fulfillment? Your Majesty, I give you the study of foot therapy and the new Anodyne Solar Powered Footbath. Your Majesty, you are my most valued audience. I want you to endorse this product- where ever the Anodyne Solar Powered Footbath is sold, everyone will associate it with Her Majesty Anne Boleyn. I could make you a full partner in my corporation. Everyone will know that you are the Royal per-sonage whose life was changed by the new Anodyne Solar Powered Footbath. I would ask Your Majesty to remove her footwear so that she may take the therapy again.

ANNE
  But what if my life doesn't need changing? *(She begins to remove her shoes.)*

PROSPERO
  Oh, but, Your Majesty- it does need changing. Let me say it this way. You are an exceptional person. You are honorable and wise, but you are sacrificing yourself for a King who cannot see. This King is blind.

ANNE
  Quite a courageous wizard to say such a thing. Oh Prospero. Why do I trust you?

PROSPERO
  (PROSPERO takes ANNE'S foot in his hands.) Your Majesty, the love that is in your soul- it is very pure, but should it not be directed toward yourself as much as toward this King? Your Majesty, are you familiar with the notion of transmutation? The study of what you may call Alchemy my Queen?

ANNE
  Yes. As for example Nicholas Flamel, the obscure 12th century Parisian scribe.

PROSPERO

Indeed. You are most well read, Your Majesty. Are you aware that mysteries made public become cheap?

ANNE

Are you talking about secrets?

PROSPERO

Yes! Most emphatically! One must not make a bed of roses for a donkey! All that we say must remain beneath the roses. True secrets of magic can only be found in the rarest of books.

ANNE

You speak of strange things, Prospero.

PROSPERO

Yes, well... I do have a purpose, Your Majesty- Your King is blind. Could you not release your resolve in certain matters to help him achieve his sight?

(GUY enters unseen and spies on them.)

ANNE

Where do you come from, Prospero?

PROSPERO

I am from the hopes and dreams of all those who wish to save you and reward your virtue, Your Majesty. I offer you a detour on the path that is your destiny.

(GUY makes a noise by accident.)

ANNE

My God! Guy? Where did you come from?

GUY

Excuse me, Madame, Your Majesty, excuse me.... *(Exits hastily.)*

ANNE

That was Guy, King Henry's servant- Oh no! He saw us, Prospero-you with my foot in your hand! Oh lord! This is a disaster! No! Stop! We must stop him! This is a disaster! Oh Prospero, what am I to do?

PROSPERO

We will simply tell the truth. The Anodyne Foot Therapy System is the most exciting product of all time. You were giving it an inspection for possible purchase. Besides Anne, think of it- what the King needs, really, more than anything else, is the Anodyne Foot Therapy System.

ANNE

Oh Prospero. This is not well.

PROSPERO

Listen, my Lady- trust me.

ANNE

Do you really think so?

PROSPERO

Yes. Anne- you'd have to agree. King Henry needs some sunshine in his life. If the sun can run this footbath, think of what else it could provide- a safe, free and clean source of energy for all people for all time. Solar power now, Anne! The rulers of the world have all missed the significance of the sun.

ANNE

I see and understand the significance of the sunshine Prospero. It is no heresy. The inner light, beyond words.

PROSPERO

Yes. You are, my Lady, wiser than most learned men indeed.

ANNE

So... foot therapy. All right, Prospero. I'll try and sell it to the King. Besides, it's my only hope, now.

PROSPERO

We will approach the King together, Anne.

ANNE

 All right. We will give it a try Prospero.

PROSPERO

 That's the spirit my Lady. That's the spirit!

(Exeunt.)

ACT 3. SCENE 2.

*(*MICHELLE *and* TOM *enter.* TOM *is still carrying the books. He approaches* MICHELLE *who is crying.)*

TOM

 You're crying. Is something wrong?

MICHELLE

 My Queen has abandoned me. It is tragic. My life has lost all meaning.

TOM

 What do you mean?

MICHELLE

 Because I told her the truth, I am now out of her favor. Never again will I hear her say that I am her best and most faithful servant, now she treats me like any other underling. And the worst of it is that she is now as good as a ghost- as good as dead. If she goes to London then nothing can save her.

TOM

 My master will do something, Michelle. He is the most incredible person I have ever met.

MICHELLE

What good is it, my pathetic little existence?

TOM

Have you considered foot therapy Michelle?

(She baulks.)

No, really!

MICHELLE

Foot therapy? Oh Monsieur- please don't talk to me right now.

TOM

No. Really Michelle, if there is anyone who can do something to help her Majesty it is my Master.

MICHELLE

No monsieur, please!

(Enter PROSPERO *and* ANNE.*)*

PROSPERO

Tom. We're going off to London, and everything is going to be alright.

ANNE

Yes Michelle. Off we go. Everything is going to be all right.

*(*ANNE *and* PROSPERO *exit.)*

MICHELLE

Well. They're in good spirits. Mon dieu. I must have faith.

(Exeunt.)

ACT 3. SCENE 3.

(Enter KING HENRY NUMBER EIGHT. GUY *approaches him.)*

GUY

My most gracious munificence- holiest of the holy. Your greatness savages my soul- such blissful glory! Such unspeakable radiance! Such immense...strength and power!

HENRY

Very good servant. Very good.

GUY

I thank my royal sovereign for sparing my life given the perfidious relations I have for his most supreme ear to hear.

HENRY

Our royal attention is upon this salacious news.

GUY

Her majesty was spotted, my most high Lord.

HENRY

(Happily.) Spotted! You mean she has the pox!

GUY

Spotted with a man.

HENRY

(Disappointed.) Oh. *(Realizes the implication.)* Oh!

GUY

I was walking down a path, and by chance I came upon the Queen, your wife. I was on my way to the village, for I was hungry. I wanted to find myself a snack, perhaps at the ale house. I know that village, I've been through it once long ago, when I first came to London... many years ago...

HENRY

> What happened to thy adulations, servant!? Is this any way to speak to your master? *(Flicks Guy's nose.)*

GUY

> *(In agony.)* Woooe. Oh most sacred Lord, your supreme wisdom changes me- I believe your most royal ear wishes to know that her majesty was seen with her foot in a strange man's hand.

HENRY

> Her foot in a strange man's hands? What strange man?

GUY

> A man, my supreme highness- I do not know. Someone I have never seen before, my most royal greatness. *(Pause.)* He looked like a Wizard.

HENRY

> A Wizard?

GUY

> Yes, my most holy of saintly lordly, lord of all lords.

HENRY

> Very good servant, very good. We shall take action!

> *(Exeunt.)*

ACT 4. SCENE 1.

(The tower of London. Enter PROSPERO, ANNE, MICHELLE *and* TOM.*)*

PROSPERO

So this is the famed Tower of London. Hello? Servants? Hello? Anyone?

(Enter GUY.*)*

Servant! Please tell His Majesty King Henry Number Eight that Prospero the Magician has arrived.

ANNE

And tell His Most Gracious Majesty that his Queen has returned.

GUY

Yes, my Lady. *(*GUY *bows and exits)*

ANNE

May God have mercy on us.

PROSPERO

Tom, Michelle- you must wait for us outside. Off you go! Skedaddle! Be gone!

TOM

Good luck, Master.

MICHELLE

God be with you, Your Majesty.

PROSPERO

Tom- give me the books.

*(*TOM *gives* PROSPERO *the books.* MICHELLE *and* TOM *exit.)*

ANNE
> Thank you so much Prospero, you are a brave man.

PROSPERO
> You are very much worth the risk Your Majesty.

> *(KING HENRY and GUY enter. ANNE falls to her knees before HENRY.)*

ANNE
> My most beloved King- give me leave to explain what you have mis-understood.

HENRY
> We perceive only treachery!

ANNE
> Your Holiness, Your Munificence- my Lord- my heart of hearts- my love. Listen to my words. My heart is weak with admiration for the most lordly of all Kings.

HENRY
> Our temper and disposition has been too lenient. Who is this Wizard?

ANNE
> A salesman, my lord- a vendor, introducing a product to me- a product beyond all compare. One which he claims holds the secrets of true happiness. I wanted to sample his product so that I might purchase one for you, my King.

HENRY
> What sort of product?

> *(ANNE rises to her feet and begins the sales pitch.)*

ANNE
> It's the new Anodyne Solar Powered Foot Therapy System.

HENRY
> Foot therapy?

ANNE

Yes, my husband. Foot therapy is a most amazing science. I know the soles of the Royal feet to be a sore topic.

HENRY

The boils on the soles of our Royal feet?

PROSPERO

Ah, yes. Septic feet.

HENRY

You dare speak thus of the Royal feet?

PROSPERO

Forgive me Your Majesty, but I am familiar with the condition- as a physician, I mean.

HENRY

You're a Wizard and a physician?

PROSPERO

Yes, I am. *(*HENRY *clears his throat.)* My most holy, most outrageously lofty King.

HENRY

Better.

ANNE

My most gracious and gentle lord- my dove. You cannot be angry- as I, your Queen, am filled with love of your most radiant soul, my sovereign, and only think of your well being. May I now present to you the creator and owner of the Anodyne Corporation?

HENRY

Our patience is wearing thin. Who is this rogue who was reportedly seen with the foot my Queen in his hands.

ANNE

Forgive me, my lord! An innocent part of the therapy, I assure you.

HENRY

He must present himself. Rapscallion!

ANNE BOLEYN

Please! I ask- I beg my gracious husband for forgiveness! It was an innocent sampling of the product. One which is meant for my husband, one which he needs- I think only of my King!

PROSPERO

O most fabulous, great King. *(Bows.)* I wish to present my product to Your Majesty, and if you don't agree that it is the most amazing product of all time- I will not be concerned! Because, my most fabulous, incredible, great King- I think you'll agree- it is the most relaxing, agreeable, most mind-blowing sensation of your lifetime!

ANNE

What could be more therapeutic than a footbath?

PROSPERO

Not just any footbath, Your Majesty! But the new Anodyne Solar Powered Foot Therapy System- a registered trademark under the Anodyne Corporation.*(Quietly.)* Extra shipping charges may apply.

HENRY

He's mad.

ANNE

No your majesty! Relief for your feet- a sore topic.

PROSPERO

Just flip the switch to the on position to start the whirlpool of warm, Epsom salt water and the patented rotating foot pads will sooth the feet in precisely programmed ways. Just find a relaxing place to sit and cast in thy feet to enjoy the warm, relaxing sensation.

ANNE

Why not add a little tea tree oil to the water, Prospero?

PROSPERO

Why not, indeed, Your Majesty! The feet are highly important- critical! My most lofty, most absorbent sovereign, think for a moment about your feet. You walk upon them- they are grounded upon the earth. Over twenty-six different bones and many more meridians make the feet a veritable conduit of the Universal Love Force Energy™. May I present Exhibit A: my foot! A miracle of creation; a microcosm, if you will. My great, incredible, colossal sovereign, it is only man and woman that can stand upright, animals are given over to gravity and to satisfying the impulses of the purely physical. Man and woman alone can lift themselves upright and reach up and back to contemplate the stars above them. This also frees the hands to be put together, right and left, to contemplate polarities and through prayer to come into consciousness and a true understanding of good and evil. I am about to go beyond our standard pitch. I, sir, am a salesman and- Your Royal most excellent Majesty- I really want to sell this product to you. You get the tea tree oil, the footbath and our special Anodyne soap and water combination, and all I ask in return Your Majesty, is the right to travel your realm to collect and preserve books.

HENRY
Books? Our patience is being stretched.

ANNE
But my Lord! My most gracious King, do the royal feet not crave relief?

HENRY
We perceive that this foot box is most untrustworthy.

ANNE
My sovereign, my precious husband- I only think of your comfort. Perhaps Prospero's wizardry could be of some assistance?

HENRY
Wizardry? Witchcraft!

PROSPERO
No! Not witchcraft- my most expansive and powerful Lord- but artful science.

HENRY
>Science?

PROSPERO
>Yes, my incredible, great, immense King. I not only bring relief for your feet. I bring you science. The new Anodyne Solar Powered Foot Therapy System has the potential- my most great lord- of making Your Majesty the most important King in all of history, because this footbath is powered by the sun. The sun, my Lord.

HENRY
>Powered?

PROSPERO
>Yes. This new Anodyne Solar Powered Footbath is the most incredible product of all time! It derives its energy from the sun and- with most profound respect and honor, my colossal sovereign- sunshine is exactly what the Royal feet desperately need.

ANNE
>If my most honored husband and wise sovereign would sample the product, I feel strongly that he would see that it really is the most amazing product of all time.

PROSPERO
>The sun- my great, expansive most powerful King- is the essence of all life. All your most incredible Majesty needs is sunshine- the sun provides knowledge. Just as the great and powerful conquer nations, the wise conquer the light of knowledge as is most properly and clearly represented in books- all books! Books, my King!

HENRY
>Books?

PROSPERO
>The sun shines light- the light of reason, and books are the light of knowledge. Without learning virtue cannot be attained. If my gracious Lord would only remove his footwear.

HENRY

Remove my footwear?

ANNE

Only to experience the most pleasant, relaxing sensation of your lifetime or your money back!

HENRY

Enough! Stop this buffoonery!

PROSPERO

Look at these books, my great King- look! Aristotle's treatise on immortality; lost works of Geoffrey Chaucer- and this obtained here in
your realm only after a short time! Your Majesty, there are hundreds
of books that need preserving in your kingdom- and yet these books
represent only a speck of the knowledge the King could conquer-
with the new life derived from the Anodyne Solar Powered Foot
Therapy System.

HENRY

We have no great love of books- excess reading loosens the mind.
Knowledge is the sin of Adam.

PROSPERO

Not so, my Lord!

HENRY

You dare contradict us?

PROSPERO

No, my most incredible, great King.

HENRY

You are to be turned into cold flesh by the word of our most Royal
will.

ANNE

No! My most gentle husband, my most loving sovereign- if you
would simply remove your footwear, you would see.

HENRY

Enough! The Royal footwear does not want removal by any means.

ANNE

My gracious husband!

HENRY

Enough! This wizard and his books have poisoned my Queen's sense. We hate books. Books are detestable. We despise books more than anything else. *(Takes the books.)* We dislike their use in our realm- they are for doctors and madmen only. We will destroy these vile pig skins!

PROSPERO

Don't!

HENRY

What?

PROSPERO

No- I'm serious. You can't do that. That's the very worst thing anyone can do! Look. That Chaucer alone, it's value can't be mea- sured!

HENRY

You dare question our will?

PROSPERO

It's just- look, you can't destroy books. They're too important.

HENRY

Servant. Take these books and toss them to the flames. *(Gives* GUY *the books.)*

PROSPERO

No!

HENRY

Our will is supreme. This Wizard must die. And his devilish foot box must be smashed and ground to pieces.

ANNE

> No! No! Please, my sweetest husband. No, I beg you. Spare him.

HENRY

> Books! What buffoonery!

PROSPERO

> Not so, great King! With my humblest supplication- please your most magnificent Lord- hear your most humble of servants. Please don't harm those books!

HENRY

> We revile all books that are the product of subjects beyond law and medicine.

PROSPERO

> Philosophy and literature, my Lord.

HENRY

> Heresy.

PROSPERO

> Not so, my Lord. Not so.

HENRY

> You dare contradict our sovereign wisdom?

PROSPERO

> Reading is the only way the mind fully grows, my Lord.

HENRY

> Yes! That is precisely why we must vigorously destroy heretical text. Servant, toss those filthy, moldy parchments to the flame.

PROSPERO

> No, your most great and magnificent King. I wouldn't do that. It would be a very grave mistake, for I- your great and bounteous, magnificent sovereign- am a mouse!

HENRY

A mouse? What! Madman! Servant! Toss those books to the flames!
(GUY burns the book.)

PROSPERO

I am a mouse, your largeness, great lard.

HENRY

Fiend! Heretic! You are to be punished and executed!

PROSPERO

If I told you that I could turn into a mouse before your very eyes,
would you fear me?

HENRY

We fear no one, Wizard. You are to be burned at the stake until dead!
You are a worshipper of devils.

PROSPERO

You don't believe I could do it?

HENRY

Turn into a mouse?

PROSPERO

A miracle- true magic. You should fear a Wizard, great, wide, cor-
pulent King. By the power of God, virtue is rewarded on earth
and in heaven. I am a mouse- and I am proud to be a mouse. I'm
not ashamed of being a mouse. And though I am a mouse, what I
really want is to be an excellent salesman and to sell you the new
Anodyne Solar Powered Foot Therapy System! Behold my true form!
(PROSPERO turns into a mouse.)

HENRY

Ahhhhhhh! A mouse! A mouse! We hate mice! We simply can't bear
them! *(Stands on a chair.)* Quick- Servant! Kill it. Kill it! Kill it! Lady
Boleyn! Stomp on it!

ANNE

It's only a mouse, my Lord.

PROSPERO

What if I told you that I could remove your head from your body, oh great, expansive King Henry Number Eight?

ANNE

Prospero! No!

PROSPERO

My lady, this magic is true. It is heavens response to you, dear, virtuous lady. I weep. Why am I in tears? Out of love, sweet and true. How to share a mouse's heart? We are soft in our deepest nature. Think, King Henry eight, what sort of journey would a real Wizard take?

HENRY

One that is evil!

PROSPERO

Not a mouse, my lord. For mice are not evil. It is only men who are evil. No time to waste. Since King Henry seems to particularly enjoy removing the heads of others let's see if it suits him. Off with his head!

(The King's head floats off of his body and grows into a large egg lying on its side. The egg should be painted white and the actors face should be projected onto the smooth curved surface of the egg.)

HENRY

AHHHHHH! My body- where is my body!

ANNE

Prospero, no! I forbid it!

(A magnificent ANGEL appears.)

PROSPERO

Do you see that Angel, Lady Boleyn?

ANNE

Yes!

PROSPERO
> Believest thou in Angels, Henry King?

HENRY
> The bible speaks of them.

PROSPERO
> What is in this Angel's hand?

HENRY
> A letter.

ANGEL
> Listen closely, Henry King Number Eight. Elizabeth is to be King.

ANNE
> What?

HENRY
> Preposterous!

ANGEL
> King Henry Number Eight, you must not harm Anne Boleyn, you must accept that Elizabeth will be King.

HENRY
> This is a Wizard's trick!

PROSPERO
> King Henry Number Eight- you would kill her majesty Anne Boleyn! You would behead her!

ANNE
> What! No, Prospero.

PROSPERO
> No? You misconstrue his majesty's will and character my Lady.

ANNE
> Nonsense. It is not true! No, my lord loves his Queen. I will bear you a

prince, Your Majesty. I know I have given you only one daughter. But I love you, my most gracious King- I will set this right. Prospero- you must put the King's head back upon his body. I beg you!

PROSPERO

Oh, sweetest of all Ladies, only your heart could be so gentle as to not see this King for the villain he is!

ANNE

No! You will not speak of my sovereign in this way. Husband, my lord, my King, forgive me. I am innocent of any transgression of heart. I will give you a prince. We can try again, husband- and I promise, I will bear you a son.

PROSPERO

My lady, you must trust me. Look upon this Angel. I am a mouse from far in your future, Anne Boleyn. It is time for me to explain. Some people love mice, others have a phobia. We are the gentlest of creatures. I have come to help you, sweet Anne- to offer you a chance to become one of us. My most gentle Queen, please hear me. I know your fate. Though you are innocent of any crime, you are beheaded on May 19, 1536 at the age of 35- by a special swordsman from Calais. Then eleven days later King Henry takes Jane Seymour as his bride.

ANNE

Henry! No!

HENRY

A lie!

ANNE

Prospero. You must reattach the Kings head.

HENRY

Heresy!

PROSPERO

No, King Henry. Not so. This convergence is unique. Take the envelope, Anne. Open it and read it and tell us what it says.

ANNE

(ANNE *opens the letter. Reading.*) You are invited to the wedding of the solar King and Queen. Please present this... mouse turd at the gate.

HENRY

A mouse turd?

PROSPERO

Yes, Henry. This mouse turd represents your soul. Even though you make people worship you, this is what you really are- and it's not good, Henry. If you were to die on this day, this is how your soul would appear to the Solar King and Queen, who judge the dead. But it is not too late. You can embrace the new Anodyne Solar Powered Foot Therapy System, a registered trademark under the Anodyne Corporation, some conditions apply. But how to treat your feet when you are only a head? It's not fun being beheaded, is it?

ANNE

Oh Prospero, you must stop this. I cannot stand this. I beg you.

PROSPERO

You are such a noble Queen. Look! The Angel beckons us. My Queen, shall we not say it truly is an Angel? See the light upon its face? See its radiance? See how it glows so sweetly? It comes as a balm for your sorrows, as an expression of love and for the safety of the Queen.

HENRY

He lies Anne.

PROSPERO

Would you doubt an Angel, Henry?

ANGEL

Bring the letter to the gate. We will make the King whole again. (ANGEL *disappears.*)

ANNE

The Angel has gone, Prospero. I don't understand.

PROSPERO

It's all quite simple. Firstly, I am a mouse. Secondly, I am a wizard. And thirdly, I am a salesman. The Anodyne concept applies equally well to the feet of mice- we are the same as humans in many ways- particularly when it comes to the Universal Love Force Energy™. We too can look up in wonder at the stars. Our feet are more sensitive than a human's feet. We have miniature, mouse-sized footbaths- it is my deep desire for you to try them. My Lady Anne Boleyn- would you become a mouse too? Examine, if you will, Exhibit A: my foot. Not just any foot, my Queen, but a mouse's foot. The foot of a mouse is one of the softest, most sensitive in the universe. Mice know and understand more than what any human might expect- even the mice around your own home are smarter, more advanced than any human being. Let me ask you this. Have you ever wondered why a mouse can send grown men, even huge animals like elephants into fits of terror? We obviously can't hurt them. It is because we send electro-magnetic waves from our brains- we can communicate on a solar spectrum, huge amounts of information at once. What can King Henry do? Overeat- and behead people?

HENRY

Insolent mouse!

PROSPERO

You don't want to be a human being, Anne. Humans think they are smart, but they are actually very dumb. Unless they embrace solar power, they will only orchestrate their own extinction and the destruction of life on earth. Unfortunately, we mice need humans to live. We evolved with them, always ahead. We can turn into anything because of the power of our electro-solar-magnetic sensory organs. But we never hurt a soul. We've scared the odd farmer or two, but that's all.

HENRY

Our Royal Heart is pounding with rage at this display of disrespect for our Royal significance!

PROSPERO

Heart? You have no heart, Henry King! You're only a head! Not so fun being beheaded, is it?

ANNE
      Prospero! This cannot be- Henry is a divine sovereign.

PROSPERO
      No, Anne. He would behead you. He knows it to be true!

HENRY
      Not so! Vicious slander!

PROSPERO
      Listen to me, my Lady- wasn't Michelle warning you? It's true. And
      now, look! How is it the King's head is off his body and a tiny mouse
      is offering you a new life? As you said, Virtue is noticed by Kings
      and by heaven! But this King would reward your Virtue by behead-
      ing you. And this mouse would reward you with full partnership in
      the Anodyne Corporation and the new Anodyne Solar Powered Foot
      Therapy System. You must leave the King! Anne, dump his fat sorry
      ass and go out with me instead!

ANNE
      No. I am devoted unto death!

PROSPERO
      Why stay with a fat, abusive creep who has no respect for you? Make
      the leap, Anne! Become a mouse like me. Mice are better. No eating
      meat, no war, no weapons of mass destruction, no murder- we have
      nice family get-togethers where everybody gets along and we don't
      hurt anything or anybody, and best of all- we are masters of Gnomic
      Foot Therapy!

TRUMPETER
      (TRUMPETER *appears and blows his horn.*) Welcome to the gate.

      (*A large scale and seven weights appear.*)

PROSPERO
      Since ancient times- when the temple was the temple of the sun-
      the Solar Power which brought life to earth, fire to the heav-
      ens- the life-giving Solar Power has given its blessing for free!
      Generosity, warmth, love, all the gifts of life- free. As simple as

lying in the sunshine. Tyrants and criminals put a price on living, taking by force the birthright of innocence. Unlike the divine example displayed daily by the Solar Power, there is no generosity in the tyrant, only selfishness and greed. Hear me now and for all time! The tyrant must ultimately pay! There is universal justice! Hear me, King Henry Number Eight- you will not escape these scales!

HENRY

What are these scales?

PROSPERO

The scales of justice have appeared. The most ancient story- the most ancient of ancient myths. The virtue of one's soul is weighed on these cosmic scales. To pass the test is to enter sweet paradise- to fail is to be barred from the Palace of the Solar King and Queen. My Lady Anne Boleyn, please sit upon the divine scales.

(She sits. The TRUMPETER blows his horn and places a feather on the other side of the scale. The feather tips the scale- it weighs more then ANNE BOLEYN.)

GUY

Look- the Queen weighs less than a feather!

PROSPERO

Proof of her Virtue. Heaven will grant her any wish.

ANNE

My wish is to restore the King. To reattach his head to his body; and also that he may have his prince, a male heir to his throne.

ANGEL

(ANGEL reappears) Your wish will be granted Anne Boleyn. Present us the letter of invitation.

(ANNE presents the letter and with a pair of tweezers the ANGEL removes the mouse turd. The TRUMPETER blows the horn and the ANGEL places the mouse turd on the scales of justice.)

ANNE

>May these dreams of yours come true my husband. Your happiness is
>my deepest wish.

>*(The King's body is restored. The egg stands up. Exit* PROSPERO *and*
>ANNE. GUY *stays as a witness.)*

ACT 5. SCENE 3.

(The scene transforms to a game show. The ANGEL *and the* TRUMPETER
are co-hosts. GUY *is the audience. The* TRUMPETER *blows his horn.)*

TRUMPETER

>Welcome to the game show we like to call "Universal Karmic
>Justice!" Today's contestant is the 16th-century tyrant and glutton
>King Henry Number Eight! Lets give him a big hand! *(Holds up
>a card that says "APPLAUSE".)* And what can our contestant win
>today Angel?

ANGEL

>Well- due to the wishes of the virtuous Lady Anne Boleyn, our King
>has a rare opportunity to transform his soul!

TRUMPETER

>Transform his soul? From what into what?

ANGEL

>From a piece of crap into gold!

TRUMPETER

>Wow! What a prize!

ANGEL

Yes! First, let's see how his soul- which presently takes the form of a mouse turd- holds up on the scales of justice against the seven deadly sins!

TRUMPETER

The seven deadly sins? What are those?

ANGEL

The seven qualities that impede spiritual progress and cause great suffering. Each one of these sins can be alchemically transformed from sin into virtue- from filth into gold! That's why our King has a rare opportunity today. Let's give him a really big hand!

(He holds up the card that says "APPLAUSE".)

First, let's see how his soul weighs in against the sin of Vanity. Drum roll please!

(Drum roll sounds. A weight is put on the scale. The mouse turd is heavier than the weight.)

He fails the test!

TRUMPETER

What is Vanity, Angel?

ANGEL

Vanity is self-love to the exclusion of others. It is said to be the fault from which all others arise. It is science without humanity and causes great suffering. It can be transformed however. It is the soil from which compassion and charity grow.

TRUMPETER

Wow. That is truly amazing!

ANGEL

This tyrant King, however, fails this test- but he is ripe for transformation.

TRUMPETER
What's next Angel?

ANGEL
Next we have Envy- the desire to possess the talents and gifts of others. It is commerce without morality and causes great suffering. It is transformed however into generosity and benevolence. Drum roll please.

(Drum roll sounds. A weight is put on the scales and doesn't tip them.)

Ohhhhh! The King fails this test miserably!

TRUMPETER
What's next Angel?

ANGEL
Next, we have Gluttony! To consume more than what one needs. It is worship without sacrifice and causes great suffering. It can be transformed however into temperance, restraint and sobriety. Drum roll please.

(Drum roll sounds. The KING'S soul is weighed against gluttony and fails.)

Ooooooo! The King fails this test miserably.

(The TRUMPETER holds up a sign that says "LAUGHTER".)

Next, we have Lust! I think we all can guess how the King will fair in this test. Lust is the inordinate craving for the pleasure of another's body. It is pleasure without conscience and it causes great suffering. It can be transformed however into love and devotion. Drum roll please.

(Drum roll sounds. The king's soul is weighed and fails again.)

Ohhhh!

(The sign for "LAUGHTER" is lifted.)

Next we have Anger! Judgment without kindness, it spurns forgiveness for hatred and it causes great suffering. It can be transformed into patience and forgiveness. Drum roll please!

(Drum roll sounds. The King fails again.)

Next we have Greed! The desire for material gain. It is wealth without work and can be transformed into discipline, justice and fairness. Drum roll please!

(Drum roll sounds. The King fails again.)

Ohhhhh! The King fails six out of seven! If he fails seven, then our studio audience will see if King Henry Number Eight's soul weighs more than all seven weights combined! Oh! A rare scoundrel! Finally we have the sin of Sloth! It is the avoidance of work and it causes great suffering. It can be transformed into fortitude, courage and endurance. Drum roll please!

(Drum rolls sounds. The King fails again.)

Ohhhhh! He fails this one too! Ladies and gentleman, we will now put all seven weights on the scales at once! Is this King really that bad? Drum roll please!

(Drum roll sounds. The King's mouse turd soul weighs more than all the weights combined.)

Ohhhhhh! All seven! This King really is... a huge piece of crap!

(The TRUMPETER *holds up the sign that says, "LAUGHTER.")*

I'd like to introduce to our studio audience tonight the multitude of Angels, everyone! And the Solar King and Queen!! Let's give them a really big hand!!!!

(The TRUMPETER *holds up the card that says, "APPLAUSE.")*

Now's the part of our show where we ask our judges, the Solar King and Queen- Does King Henry Number Eight get invited to the Solar

Wedding? No! No! He doesn't. No way!!

(The TRUMPETER *holds up a card that says, "BOO".)*

Boooo! Boo!

PROSPERO
*(*PROSPERO, *back in human form, enters.)* Wait! I, Prospero the Wizard, ask the judges- May I try one more time to sell him the new Anodyne Solar Powered Foot Therapy System!

ANGEL
Hurray! Solar Power!

(The TRUMPETER *holds up a card that says, "HURRAY! SOLAR POWER!")*

PROSPERO
Your Majesty- May I call you Hank? Listen, where you from Hank?

HENRY
London.

PROSPERO
And what do you do for a living, Hank?

HENRY
I'm the King.

PROSPERO
Of London?

HENRY
No. Of England.

PROSPERO
Really! Well, let's give him a really big hand everyone! Hank, I want to sell you on this new product, Hanky baby. You have a choice. You could turn your soul into gold by choosing the egg- or you can choose to drink this cup of forgetfulness and go back and be King-

but your soul will remain a little piece of crap and upon your death will descend into darkness. What does he win if chooses the egg, Angel?

ANGEL

Why, it's the new Anodyne Solar Powered Foot Therapy System! That's right! Just flip the switch to the on position to start the whirl-pool of warm, Epsom salt water, add some of Anodyne's compli-mentary tea tree oil, cast in thy feet and enjoy the pleasant, relaxing sensation. The rotating foot pads will give you the most pleasant, most relaxing foot massage of your life- Guaranteed! And best of all, it's solar powered!

(The TRUMPET *holds up the card that says, "HURRAY! SOLAR POWER!")*

PROSPERO

Is this product safe, Angel?

ANGEL

Absolutely! This product is as safe as milk. Examine, if you will, Exhibit A: my foot! A miracle of creation. Over twenty-seven bones and many meridians make the foot a veritable conduit for the Universal Love Force Energy™.

PROSPERO

Wow. That really is amazing!

ANGEL

The Anodyne Corporation is the answer!

PROSPERO

Hank, even the Angels like this product! Wow! Hank, I want you to think about the power of making this one simple decision. You could change your eternal life today just by making a single decision. Wow. Are you excited?

HENRY

I suppose.

PROSPERO
>Got anyone you'd like to say hello to, Hank?

HENRY
>Not really.

PROSPERO
>All right then! Drum roll please.

>*(Drum roll sounds.)*

>What'll it be, Hank? Do you choose wisdom, vigilance, sobriety, courage, generosity living as another soul in paradise? Or, continue being a piece of crap, but living as King of England? Which will it be, Hank? Before you decide I want you to think about one thing. What is destiny, Hank?

>*(*KING *doesn't respond.)*

>Character! Character is destiny! Remember that: Character is destiny.

>*(*HENRY *hesitates, goes to the cup, and then drinks as* PROSPERO *speaks.)*

>Because of Anne's wish you will have a son, Edward, and he will sit as a boy upon the throne; but he will be sickly and die young and Elizabeth will be King.

ACT 3: SCENE 3.

(As HENRY lowers the cup the scene transforms back to London. GUY is standing beside him holding a cage with two white mice inside.)

GUY

We're back in the tower! Majesty! We're back! We're back!

HENRY

Servant! Take those mice away from our Royal sight! *(Flicks him in the nose.)*

GUY

Oooooo! Owwwww! My Lord. Don't you remember?

HENRY

Silence servant! Where is Lady Boleyn?

GUY

Where is Lady Boleyn?

(Looks nervously at the cage.) Right- where is Lady Boleyn? *(Looks away from the cage deliberately.)*

Uh... you beheaded her, my most wondrous, sacred King. A special swordsman was brought from Calais. *(Pause.)* But of course you remember that, don't you, your Majesty?

HENRY

Yes. So it was. Yes. Well. Servant, go you to Jane Seymour and tell her that her King will soon arrive. Be gone and tarry not! Away!

(Lights go to black.)

ACT 4. SCENE 1.

(Outside the tower. GUY *approaches* TOM *and* MICHELLE.*)*

TOM

Good servant, have you news from my Master?

GUY

Here. Take these two mice. What has happened, I cannot explain-but these two mice, they are very special.

MICHELLE

Tell me servant. What has happened?

GUY

I will tell you, but you won't believe. Your Master turned into a mouse right before my eyes!

TOM

Yes?

GUY

An Angel appeared and brought us to Saint Peter's Gate!

TOM

Really?

GUY

Truly! They weighed the King's soul, which was a mouse turd, against all seven deadly sins. And even though the mouse turd was small, it weighed more than all seven sins together.

MICHELLE

The King's soul is a turd?

GUY

Yes.

MICHELLE

Well... yes, that makes sense.

GUY

And then we were back and I was holding this cage with these two mice- and I swear- it is the Wizard and the Queen.

MICHELLE

But where is my Lady? Is she safe?

GUY

Well. Yes.

MICHELLE

In the Tower- is she in the Tower of London?

GUY

No.

MICHELLE

Then where? May I go to her?

GUY

But- she's right here!

MICHELLE

Where?

GUY

Right here. *(Holding the cage.)*

MICHELLE

Those mice?

GUY

Yes.

MICHELLE

What about those mice! Where is my Lady? I must see her- she is my life.

TOM

> She's right here, Michelle.

MICHELLE

> Present my Lady to me. My heart is a pit of darkness.

TOM

> She's here, Michelle. Look. Here.

MICHELLE

> Oh, sir, you are such an ass! Are you saying this mouse is my Lady Anne?

TOM

> Yes!

MICHELLE

> Fools! I'll smash these mice! Such nonsense!

TOM

> Don't! Michelle- he's saved her. We will release them.

MICHELLE

> What am I to do now? I feel so lost. My whole worldview has shifted. My belief system is shattered. Perhaps it is true. Could it be true?

GUY

> Listen. You two are in danger- you must leave and never come to London again! You must leave.

TOM

> You're right! Let's go, Michelle! Let's take these mice and go.

MICHELLE

> But, where? Where is there to go?

TOM

> Well- we could go to my house. It's not too far away. And I have lots of turnips and cabbages.

GUY
>Be gone, you two! Away!

TOM
>Good-bye! Thank you for your help.

>*(TOM and MICHELLE exit. Black out.)*

ACT 3. SCENE 4.

(Enter TOM and MICHELLE. They are inside Tom's house.)

MICHELLE
>This house is your home?

TOM
>Yes. It's not much, but it's mine.

MICHELLE
>Well, I suppose it's not so bad. It's... cozy.

TOM
>Would you like some ale?

MICHELLE
>All right. Why not? *(TOM pours her some ale.)* These mice- look! They seem to really like each other. And I've grown to like them. They're cute!

TOM

>They're happy to be alive. We must release them. The one is my master Prospero and the other is your Lady Anne Boleyn.

MICHELLE

>Could it really be true?

TOM

>Michelle, it is true. Who are you to say it couldn't be possible? Perhaps my Master knows a thing or two that you don't.

MICHELLE

>It's most amazing. Look- they seem so content.

TOM

>They're lucky they have each other. Life's not so hard when you're not alone. When you can find someone to share your time with- don't you think so? Let's release them.

MICHELLE

>I've been alone for so much in my life. Something is telling me it's time to stop being so alone. Good-bye little mice, good luck to you. *(They release the mice.)*

TOM

>There they go. Goodbye Master, thank you for all you have done. I will miss you. I feel so different now that I've met my Master. Foot therapy has really changed my life, Michelle. It's really amazing.

MICHELLE

>Foot therapy? I know I said it was stupid. I know I can't believe I'm saying it but, yes. I see some value in foot therapy. Especially right now. My poor aching feet!

TOM

>The feet are really, truly amazing, Michelle. Over twenty-seven different bones and many meridians make the feet a veritable conduit for the Universal Love Force Energy™.

MICHELLE

I don't know. I don't know what to believe anymore.

TOM

Well, my master did teach me a little bit about the foot. Would you like to try a foot massage Michelle?

MICHELLE

Try what?

TOM

A foot massage?

MICHELLE

No. I couldn't.

TOM

Free your feet, Michelle. Take them out of those strange shoes, and go barefoot. It feels great.

MICHELLE

Remove my footwear!

TOM

Yes! Look. It feels good!

MICHELLE

(Laughs) You're wiggling your toes.

TOM

Come on- wiggle your toes along with me. Look at my foot. Wiggle wiggle wiggle. It's fun.

MICHELLE

All right- I'll give it a try. *(Slowly removes her shoes.)*

TOM

That's the spirit! Take off your strange footwear and feel the touch of the earth. That's it! Now, let me take those feet into my hands and give them a massage.

MICHELLE
>*(*MICHELLE *pulls away.)* A foot massage?

TOM
>Yes- absolutely! Nothing could be more natural. Give it a go- Come on!

MICHELLE
>*(Yielding.)* I've never had a foot massage. I've barely let any man touch me, but something is telling me it might be time to change.

TOM
>Well, my lady. May I please have the honor of being the first to pamper you the way you should be pampered?

MICHELLE
>That's a sweet thing to say Tom.

TOM
>Come on. *(Takes her foot. She lets him. He massages her foot.)*

MICHELLE
>Ohhhhhhh! That feels really good.

TOM
>Didn't I tell you?

MICHELLE
>Oh yes. I could get used to this.

TOM
>So could I, Michelle. So could I. *(Winks at the audience. Lights fade to black.)*

EPILOGUE

(In the darkness, we hear the voices of LITTLE GIRL *and* PROSPERO.*)*

LITTLE GIRLS VOICE
That's one of my favorite stories Daddy.

PROSPERO
Well be a good mouse and go to sleep sweetie.

LITTLE GIRLS VOICE
I will. Good night Daddy.

PROSPERO
Good night sweetie. Sweet dreams.

(The end.)

Production Notes: This play could be staged in many ways, with actors, with puppets or marionettes. Clearly there are some unique staging challenges involved and any and all creative solutions are encouraged. As the author, I would only like to say that it would make me very sad if any mice were hurt or abused because of this play.

We hope you've enjoyed the stories.
Please help us share this story with other readers by letting us know what you thought with a review on either **amazon.com** or **goodreads.com**.

Thank you kindly,
Montag Press Collective

John Wojewoda is a Toronto based writer and musician who has been writing and playing music for many years. He majored in Theater at Concordia University in Montreal, and also holds a B.A. in History. Currently he is working toward a music degree from the Royal Conservatory of Music, studying classical guitar and viola. John has produced several of his own plays professionally in Toronto and Montreal. He continues to write and is currently writing a novel online called *The Reincarnation of Robert Hooke*.

www.ingramcontent.com/pod-product-compliance
Lightning Source LLC
Chambersburg PA
CBHW021054090426
42738CB00006B/326